Seizing Power

Other Titles From New Falcon Publications

Shaping Formless Fire
Taking Power
    By Stephen Mace
Undoing Yourself With Energized Meditation
The Psychopath's Bible: For the Extreme Individual
    By Christopher S. Hyatt, Ph.D.
What You Should Know About the Golden Dawn
The Golden Dawn Audio CDs
    By Israel Regardie
Ceremonial Magic and the Power of Evocation
Kabbalistic Cycles & the Mastery of Life
    By Joseph Lisiewski, Ph.D.
PsyberMagick: Advanced Ideas in Chaos Magick
The Chaos Magick Audio CDs
    By Peter Carroll
Condensed Chaos: An Introduction to Chaos Magick
The Pseudonomicon
    By Phil Hine
The Infernal Texts
    By Stephen Sennitt
Beyond Duality: The Art of Transcendence
    By Laurence Galian
Monsters & Magical Sticks: There's No Such Thing As Hypnosis?
    By Steven Heller, Ph.D.
Astrology & Consciousness
    By Rio Olesky
The Pathworkings of Aleister Crowley
    By Aleister Crowley
Astrology, Aleister & Aeon
    By Charles Kipp
Cosmic Trigger: Final Secret of the Illuminati
    By Robert Anton Wilson
An Insider's Guide to Robert Anton Wilson
    By Eric Wagner
Info-Psychology
    By Timothy Leary, Ph.D.
Join My Cult!
    By James Curcio
Zen Without Zen Masters
    By Camden Benares

Please visit our website at http://www.newfalcon.com

Seizing Power

Reclaiming Our Liberty Through Magick

by
Stephen Mace

NEW FALCON PUBLICATIONS
TEMPE, ARIZONA, U.S.A.

Copyright © 2006 by Stephen Mace

All rights reserved. No part of this book, in part or in whole, may be reproduced, transmitted, or utilized, in any form or by any means, electronic or mechanical, including photocopying, recording, or by any information storage and retrieval system, without permission in writing from the publisher, except for brief quotations in critical articles, books and reviews.

International Standard Book Number: 1-56184-239-7
Library of Congress Catalog Card Number: 2005929466

First Edition 2006

To contact the Author write to:
Stephen Mace
P.O. Box 256
Milford, CT 06460-0256
U.S.A.

Those expecting a reply should enclose a stamped, self-addressed envelope. Foreign correspondents should enclose international reply coupons.

The paper used in this publication meets the minimum requirements of the American National Standard for Permanence of Paper for Printed Library Materials Z39.48-1984

Address all inquiries to:
NEW FALCON PUBLICATIONS
1739 East Broadway Road #1-277
Tempe, AZ 85282 U.S.A.
(or)
320 East Charleston Blvd. #204-286
Las Vegas, NV 89104 U.S.A.
website: http://www.newfalcon.com
email: info@newfalcon.com

For Hal von Hofe

Table of Contents

Introduction 9
Hierarchy vs. Consensus 11
The Karma-Kulture Krisis 19
Hierarchy: A Ready Brain for the New Demiurge 33
Text and Ontology 49
For Those Who Would Subvert the Status Quo 77
Rising Through the Decline: A Magickal Look at
    Oswald Spengler 103
Bibliography 169
About the Author 173

Introduction

First I must correct a possible misinterpretation of the title. That is to say, this book has nothing to do with the overthrow or subversion of the State. The Civil State will be ours for the foreseeable future because there is going to be no miraculous transformation of human nature in the foreseeable future. For all practical purposes, the State shall be with us always.

The enemy that you will find in this text has nothing to do with princes or presidents, except to the extent they be wholly-owned subsidiaries of our true foes. Our true nemesis is instead corpocracy. This is rule by an institutional oligarchy, a plutocracy not of rich people but of "limited liability corporations"—machines, in essence, that produce wealth without regard for human values except to the extent that a mimicking of these is necessary to maintain political control.

Now by "limited liability corporation" I neither include nor condemn those individuals, families and partnerships who must incorporate for legal survival. Who knows, perhaps someday there may even need to be a Stephen Mace, Inc. But the day I choose to go public, and sell stock, shoot me! And not as a charlatan or thief, either, but as one who would subcontract his soul to the stockholders, who would steer his will by share price, who would submit his integrity to judgment by the marketplace. To do so would make me something other than human, a condition that is today all too common. The control of charlatans and thieves is the business of the State. Resistance to soul-sucking vampires requires an entirely different level of activity.

But lest I imply that the fault lies all beyond us, I begin this book with a chapter on the politics we find within magickal groups. The better we can get along with each other, the more coherent will be our power for use against our true foes.

Hierarchy vs. Consensus

The word "hierarchy" comes from the Greek word meaning "a steward of sacred rites"—namely, the guy who went to school to learn what's holy. This is a perfectly sensible career path for those who are working within a long-standing tradition, for if a tradition is to be kept alive, it requires a well-educated leadership to perpetuate all the symbolic nuances woven throughout its ritual and political fabric. Here a dedicated hierarchy, devoted to the preservation of the system, assiduously applying the accumulated wisdom to the work of each generation, can be essential if the wisdom is to survive.

Historically, the most successful hierarchy of all has been the Roman Church. In the realm of the occult, the O.T.O. would have to take that place. To the Catholics the hierarchy is justified by the need to preserve the "true" sacrament so it might be ministered to the millions of faithful around the world. In the O.T.O.'s case there is the need to train initiates in the delicate matter of sexual alchemy, and also for a continuing study of the complexities of the Enochian system. Both these goals can be helped by institutional support, and those who wish to pursue them could do well to consider an affiliation.

But this has nothing to do with anything I ever thought Chaos magick was supposed to be about.

All parties agree that the principle inspiration for the Chaos current was the life and work of Austin Osman Spare. Spare is well-known both for his conspicuous power (making rain, reading minds, etc.) and also his insistence that we map out the salient features of our own spiritual clusters if we are to use power efficiently. Rather than going to school to learn what's holy, we each of us must decide it for ourselves, and this helps to define our wills. The beauty of Spare's whole approach is that we each of us must plunge down into our own creativity and exploit it for whatever power we are able to master.

There are, of course, many special skills we must learn if we are to be successful here—the practices of sigil design, trance, conjuration, meditation, divination and all the other methods for wrestling with power and mastering it. But our training in these need not depend upon our submission to some order. Apart from what we may read in books, much of our instruction may be left "to chance," this allowing for the freest possible play of power in omen, astral work, and conjuration. In the context of power, the whispered confidence of a pathological liar can be more relevant and useful than the sworn truth of the most respectable authority. Only in the case of a direct apprenticeship can a long-lasting student-teacher relationship be justified, and here the link must be so truly personal that no written agreement is required. Any formalization of the connection would limit it, an interference that both master and student would instantly reject. But only if a teacher is committed to giving such individual attention can he or she expect any kind of allegiance on the part of the student. For a hierarchy of teachers to extract money or magickal support from a *group* of students, when the mysteries taught are already hidden within the students' own souls, is rank parasitism of the "upper" upon the "lower," regardless of how much power the teachers actually possess.

This is not to say that group work should be avoided. If a number of wizards can work together so their energies amplify each other without interference, they will surely benefit from their alliance. But they must be as together as a string quartet if they are to generate harmony and not discord. In hierarchy such unity is generated from the top down. If we reject this, what is our alternative?

The most obvious solution is simply for everyone to get together and agree on a course of action—that is, to come to a consensus and then follow it. But this alternative, though clearly superior if we can succeed at it, is by no means easy to establish or maintain. Unlike hierarchy, where there is a predetermined ladder which the ambitious may aspire to climb, the politics in a consensual arrangement are freeform and can range from the useful to the grotesque. Much here depends on the specifics of the group's membership and the nature of its purpose. We will try to examine some of the variables and suggest ways of dealing with the more likely difficulties before they arise.

The clearest problem, and also the most tedious and mundane, is the maintenance of discipline. By this I do not mean making people toe the line, but simply having people do what they've agreed to do when they've agreed to do it. Without this personal commitment to carrying out plans once the group has made them, the unity needed to generate true magickal intensity will be impossible to achieve.

In hierarchal arrangements discipline comes almost naturally. Of course it's in the nature of hierarchy for responsibility to increase as one climbs the ladder, an ascension that should be prevented by those above if one below were unreliable in matters of magick. Also, a committed elite that runs things is much better able to prune dead wood than a group as a whole. They have the *authority* to throw people out, and so discipline of the lower ranks can be executed with a certain swift grace.

Except in unusually clear-cut circumstances, the spirit of consensus forbids such efficiency. By definition consensus is a general agreement, and a general agreement on an expulsion would include the consent of the one expelled. And even if everybody gets together behind his or her back and decides among themselves, there will likely be other members who work hard enough but who are friends of the miscreant, and who don't wish to jeopardize their relationships by consenting to the expulsion. So no general agreement will be possible, and only a resort to a majority vote will suffice.

Majority voting is a rather glaring violation of consensual working, and in fact things rarely come to this. What usually happens is either the workers carry the slackers and the magick suffers accordingly, or else the workers drop out of the group, leaving the slackers and their friends in their misery, and then form a new group on their own. This second option takes a great deal of spine, including the ability to keep one's gossip to oneself, but its successful accomplishment is a great boost to group momentum. It's much easier on the social life than any direct confrontation, too.

This method of disbanding and then reforming works well against almost any undesirable faction, even if it happens to be the majority. If a spiritual fad for, say, enlightenment through self-flagellation sweeps the group, those with enough sense to know it for what it is can simply not show up anymore, and go off on their own to work as their good sense dictates.

Of course one way to avoid these troubles is to admit only mature magickal personalities into one's company, thus keeping away those who are susceptible to fads, but this seems to work against both the health of the group and the spiritual progress of the human species. Without the fresh views of a variety of neophytes, some of whom may possess innate powers that could stimulate the research of even the most advanced, groups inevitably turn gray and stagnate. That is, to teach is also to learn. And if advanced magicians neglect their obligation to teach, inspire, and give example, what will give the new time the *thrust* to overcome the inertia of the old? The current of the aeon may be in our favor, but if we do not apply it with a will, the rot of patriarchy may still engulf us.

This is not to say that a group should admit just anyone. If a person is conspicuously neurotic or unreliable, there is no reason not to repeatedly lose, with deep regret, his or her phone number, and simply never have time to write. But if we insist that all our candidates be so well known that there is no chance we will ever wish to be rid of one, we may lose some promising prospects and come off looking like snobs in the bargain.

The solution I would propose here is a modified hierarchy, one made up of an inner and an outer order, each run by the consensus of its members, with the only authority of the inner order being that of deciding when to admit members of the outer into its ranks.

Adepts from the inner could, upon request, attend the meetings of the outer to advise, inspire, and leave if requested. The inner could staff classes in which the members of the outer could enroll if they wished. In return, the inner would have a reserve of potential recruits close at hand, where their magickal progress could be encouraged and their personal power and ability to take responsibility observed.

There is one last function of group dynamics that we should consider—the interaction of introverts and extroverts. It is an inevitable complication, as unavoidable as human psychology, and one big reason why it's difficult to keep consensual organizations together for any period of time. In short, if the interaction is not recognized and specifically addressed, *de facto* hierarchies tend to emerge, pecking orders whose top spots carry all the authority a formal hierarchy provides, but with none of the constitutional restraints.

The introvert/extrovert dichotomy was first formalized by the Swiss psychologist Carl Gustav Jung. Briefly, Jung saw extroverts as those who tend to recognize other people and external objects and events as the decisive things in life, while introverts consider their interior psychic states to be more important. Extroversion taken to an extreme tends to get people swallowed in externals, neglecting their inner necessities in favor of a reflexive adaptation to their environments. Introversion taken to an extreme loses touch with what is real.

In consensus arrangements, the introvert-extrovert interaction makes itself most apparent in the process of planning. Consensual planning involves everybody getting together at once and deciding *what* they are going to *do*. But the *whats* are always external and the *dos* usually are, or at least the ones people have to agree about at meetings. So the extroverts are in their element, and the introverts out of theirs. Since meetings are where authority is claimed and maintained, if the extroverts get to like deciding what's going to happen, and the introverts let them, they can become the leadership just out of habit. If the extroverts get along well enough to divide the power effectively, an oligarchy will result. If they don't, those with less taste for followers will depart, leaving the introverts under the wing of the most self-inflated—a grand guru with everything but the power.

To keep this sort of pathology from getting a toehold, close attention must be paid to the decision-making process and each member's participation in it. Also, it must be clear to all that each member has an obligation to participate in the process, in one way or another.

One important point is that no one can be designated introvert or extrovert. The roles change frequently with the situations encountered. Someone who's mouselike at meetings may bull in and take over when it comes time to make a fire. The simplest thing is just to say that we ourselves know which we are in any specific circumstance, and from this standpoint may we propose steps to safeguard the consensual state.

The one I offer (just as an idea, quite untested) is a head-on confrontation with the introvert/extrovert dichotomy, an incorporation of it into the decision-making process. Given a proposition, each member of a group would decide whether he or she felt extroverted or introverted about it—that is, whether he or she felt challenged to address it or preferred to wait and see what the other members had to say about it first. They would then divide into two groups, the extroverts working out a consensus on what should be done, leaving the introverts to the refreshments. When the extroverts had put together something they all liked, they would present it to the introverts, who could then work out how they all felt about it while the extroverts had their turn at the milk and cookies. When the introverts had agreed they liked it or decided why they didn't, they would get back together with the extroverts to produce a final consensus.

To close I would like to stress one final point: consensus takes time. To ignore the subtle nuances of group interaction in favor of getting a meeting over with is to jeopardize the success of the magick. To create *de facto* leaders for the sake of efficiency is to jeopardize both consensus and everyone's (including the leaders') spiritual growth. People who want leaders should join hierarchal orders—if, that is, they have any business doing magick at all. In the end, each magician must be a King, and an alliance of Kings is an alliance of equals. There is no room for leaders there.

First published in *Chaos International* no. 4, Leeds, 1988.

The Karma-Kulture Krisis

I. No Place to Rest

According to Classical Hindu thinking, any act performed with desire will result in an accumulation of karma, which is simply a tendency to believe that fulfillment of desire is a worthwhile thing to achieve. This belief traps us in the round of birth, death and rebirth because desire can only be fulfilled if we possess a body of flesh, and so after death we will seek a new body out of habit. The traditional yogic means for escaping this cycle is by renouncing all experience, this to be done through meditation and asceticism. The Hindu theistic counter to this, as presented in the *Bhagavad-Gita*, is that the desire to achieve liberation is as binding as any other, especially when the method for attaining it involves such extreme austerities. Its solution was for us to recognize our places in society and then do our duties to them without any sort of personal attachment. Warriors should fight, craftsmen should fabricate, haulers of dung should haul dung, and by leaving aside all ambition beyond a disciplined devotion to the work, desire can be nullified and liberation achieved. But this can be difficult to accomplish unless one is already in settled circumstances, so the *Gita* suggests that one should also live for the sake of the Deity, in this case Krishna, devoting all one's acts to him and thus removing self as a matter of concern.

This devotional approach to spiritual liberation works well in any settled society, and is the paradigm for Christianity as well as bhakti yoga. The Christian devotes self to spouse, children and church, with the Risen Christ as his or her ongoing inspiration. So long as he or she can find a stable role in his or her culture, it is surely possible to lose self in this way, accomplishing a karmic cleansing even as karma is misidentified as sin. For the sincere devotee the effects are equivalent.

Now for the twenty-five or so centuries before this one, this aspiration to karma-free devotion was about all that was available in the way of spiritual paths within the civilized world. In tribal cultures the way to power was by accessing the natural web of power that made up the local ecosystem, but when the power came to be channeled through a civic organization, devotion to the deity that was the guardian of that channel was the only way to go. Even the early pioneers of Western magick, heretics to the Christian Church, can be seen as operating in this devotional mode. Bruno, Campanella, Dee and the first Rosicrucians were all working to bring the power down more efficiently so a more heavenly civic order might be established on earth. Their differences with orthodoxy were matters of symbolism and technique, not intent.

Of course then as now there were plenty of unspiritual paths one could choose to take through life. Devotion to hedonism, commerce and political power were all options, if one's status at birth gave one any options at all. But even if one chose simply to amass wealth, the ideal of devotion was still there to curb conspicuous displays of rapacity. And to those who truly desired the divine, the life of devotion was available, approved and easy to fall into. The devotee became the instrument of the Divine Order within the civic order that was the reflection of the Divine Order on earth, and so became free of all desire, save that for the divine.

In the course of our miserable century, however, the order of society has vanished like a flower in a flood, and the muck that has replaced it, wide-open as it is, is in no way conducive to any sort of service to one's place in life. The economic situation is so turbulent that it is next to impossible to lose self in devotion to one's work. Even the best craftsman will starve without marketing—which is the art and science of manipulating desire—and the worker who tries to remain above the politics of the workplace is soliciting redundancy. As for national politics, the rise of "democracy" has bleached the last vestige of the divine from out of the civic order, and the person who puts his or her faith in lawful government might as well admit that in reality that faith is in cold, hard cash. Money buys media time, media consultants and media focus groups, and media exposure is what makes a candidate acceptable to that ever-shrinking proportion of the population that actually believes that voting matters. Laws come not from a consensus of the people but from a consensus of the special interests that have bought and paid for the parliaments of the world. Justice is available only to those who can afford it.

With the civic order thus corrupted, it is no surprise that the traditional means of shedding karma through devotion have turned rancid. Western culture has become so anti-religious—so wrapped up in wealth and power, status and lust—that for the average Christian Jesus has become a mere product to be purchased. For the truly devout, on the other hand, there is almost an obligation to struggle against the culture. But this forces one to become involved in it in the most negative way possible, ensuring that one will become entangled in karma and sin both. Take the crusaders against "Satanic Child Abuse," for instance.[1] They see sin everywhere, which is not an entirely inaccurate perception, and their Biblical training tells them it must be from us pagans. So they sic the gutter press on us, and in this way tar themselves to sin's main modern source—the putrid commercialism of the mass media. Hopelessly stuck to it, they will go down with it, unable to see the

---

[1] During the 1980's and early 90's in Britain, and to some small extent in the United States, the right wing of Christian Fundamentalism produced the theory that children were being born into covens so they could be sexually abused and even sacrificed to Satan. The only evidence for this was memories "recovered" by hypnosis from "victims" whose families and long-time associates had no idea of what they were talking about. This lack of corroboration and the utter absence of physical evidence meant the police were usually uninterested, but that didn't stop the Fundies from whipping Britain's gutter press into an hysterical campaign against pagans, resulting in some arson, a lot of commercial and employment discrimination, and even British social service agencies removing children from pagan families.

god within and around us, but only the projection of their own fear onto what they are too narrow-minded to understand. Their religion is obsolete, so even if their hearts are pure, their methodology will fail them. At the height of its power, their god was the king in heaven who was the spiritual equivalent of the king on earth. But with the change in time this ideal has become too archaic to return the power its believers need to sustain their devotions. A new methodology is required, and one look at the degeneration of modern culture assures us that the need is urgent.

Back before the Salvationist theology of Christianity won its victory in the West, the ideal of devotion to a transcendent Good received its most rigorous treatment at the hands of the Greek philosopher Plato. From his work there developed an ethic of otherworldliness that permeated Classical culture, one that Christianity took on almost in its entirety. But there was one aspect of Platonism that the Christians did not accept, the notion of the transmigration of souls, which is simply another term for reincarnation. The Neoplatonist philosopher Plotinus, for instance, believed that the soul descends from the undifferentiated Absolute One and can find bliss only if it turns back to it. But since soul is incarnated in a body of flesh, it is also able to manipulate the things of sense, embodied in Matter, which Plotinus saw as the epitome of evil. To the extent that we turn away from Matter and back to the One, he felt that we would come to a more exalted life next time around. But if we involve ourselves in Matter, Matter will pull us down farther in our subsequent incarnations, ultimately causing our souls to become embodied as rats and roaches, mold and slime.

During its passed age of health and vigor, Western society was set up to at least allow for an aspiration to something higher than a blind pursuit of material glamour, but no longer. Our economies keep up their mad pace through an ongoing conjuration of greed; our politicians keep their power through fear; and a full-voice chorus of greed and fear, rut and horror is how the mass media earn their bread and butter. To give them our attention is to play their game, to be sucked into a maelstrom heading down, down to a world were greed and fear attain their apotheosis. If we fall with them, if we let them use our power to define the world to come, then Nature will be raped and made whore, all spirit will leave her, and there will be places on earth only for rats and roaches, mold and slime.

II. The Dual Principle as Demiurge

In Gnostic theology the Demiurge was a lesser divinity of limited knowledge and much malice who was responsible for the creation of the universe. Through some ruse or another (depending on sect), he was able to trap sparks of the Absolute Light within his malicious clockwork. These sparks are the souls of us humans, and thus encased in our fleshy bodies we are blind to our origins in the Unlimited. The gnosis (knowledge) of the various sects was an awareness of our divine origins and the technique we could use to escape, either in trance or upon death, back to our homes in the Light. This escape is perilous, however, since the Demiurge wants to keep us enslaved and has positioned Archons (Rulers) as guards at each of the seven spheres we must pass through on our ways up and out.

The dual principle, on the other hand, is a philosophical concept first formulated by the English wizard Austin Osman Spare. Briefly, it holds that by the very act of believing one thing, we make its opposite equally necessary. If we believe in "up," there must be a "down." If we believe in "creation," there must be "destruction." If we believe in "love," there must be "hate." And the stronger the belief, the stronger must be the inevitable reaction. Thus the one who gives all for love may react with murder when the beloved seeks to escape from such neurotic clinging. Thus the State that demands order and obedience conjures chaos and rebellion by the oppressive nature of its enforcement.

In this way Spare saw the dual principle as a mechanism by which desire entraps us, a consequence of desire that locks us into Matter as securely as any Demiurge. Thus he gives us a more detailed dynamic for karmic encrustation than that offered by the

Hindus. To desire anything is to conjure its opposite even as it is obtained, ensuring that desire will become a never-ending state of struggle.

But if the dual principle dominates the phenomenal world, and thus serves as Demiurge, what is the Light beyond? For Spare, it is Kia. Kia is a typical formless Absolute like the Ain Soph or Tao or the One of Plotinus. Unlike the Gnostics, however, Spare did not see Kia as being in opposition to the dual principle, but rather the dual principle as being Kia's tool to carry out its purpose of Self-love. As in Crowley's Thelema, Spare held that the universe is the means the Absolute uses to enjoy itself—the toy of its cosmic hedonism. By using the dual principle to simulate opposition, Kia divides "I" from "Self"—the point of view from the things perceived—and so spawns organic life. As Spare wrote in his *Book of Pleasure*, "In fear all creation pays homage, but does not extol its [Kia's] moral, so everything perishes unbeautifully." (p. 8) Its moral is Self-love, "Self" for Spare being anything we can perceive, "the negation of completeness as reality," the only thing sufficiently all-encompassing to transcend the dual principle and claim True Existence. For the solipsistical Spare, Self is the equivalent of Nuit, and love for it is the only way to escape the trap of the dual principle. Thus Spare offers a pantheistic hedonism as an improvement on the more traditional theistic devotional path, for though the dynamic is similar, the object of devotion has been expanded to include infinity. Through Self-love we match our momentums with Kia's and draw its power, though of course to do this requires that we purge ourselves of whatever might limit our ability to perceive Kia's totality—that is, "all we believe." The dual principle is only a snare if we allow the extremes it defines to attract or repel us. If we refrain from belief in them, they are only the separate steps of a dance, insignificant in the context of the whole.

Unfortunately, there exist politically powerful people whose continuing prosperity depends upon the ongoing dominance of the dual principle over all aspects of society. By giving up beliefs smaller than Self-love and thus freeing ourselves from duality, we free ourselves from the mechanisms this power elite uses to perpetuate its grip on culture, for belief is the tool it uses to keep us enthralled. To keep profits high it needs us to believe that possessions define our self-worth, that money buys love, that pleasure is equivalent to consumption. To keep governments in power it needs us to believe that order comes from law, that ethics come from morals, that self-identity depends on national identity. To discard these illusions even as we use our rejection as a means for accessing power is to put their whole edifice in peril, and so to conjure the wrath of their most powerful archon, the mass media. AND YET WE MUST PERSIST! The fate of our fair planet depends on it.

III. The Media as Archon

To the Gnostics the Archons were, in general, the personified planets. Arrayed in seven concentric spheres around the central earth, they managed events here with total Fatality and, through these events, confined humanity's consciousness to the narrow parameters they defined. Their most important task was never to allow people to have any notion of their divine origins. It was only through the sacrifice of the Messenger from outside the prison clockwork (often identified with Jesus) that this awareness was obtained, along with the magickal knowledge needed to overcome the Archons as one met each of the seven on the way out.

In our present day the way to overcome the Archons is simply not to buy the lies they print on paper, and to switch off the bloody tube. But even as we do so, they strive to whip our neighbors into a frenzy against us, for if the knowledge we thus gain should get out, their whole clockwork could fall apart, and the knowledge of the Light become universal.

The Gnostics and Plotinus both had it wrong. The evil lies neither in the planets nor in Matter, but within small minds. They know only the dual principle and thus can see only the banalities of extreme opinion, never the Self-love that soars above it. But extreme opinion is required to conjure emotion, and emotion entertains, and entertainment sells. It sells newspapers; it sells advertising; it sells movie tickets; it sells politicians. Thus it is the media's bread and butter, the consciousness they must continuously evoke if they are to continue their hypertrophied existence. If humankind should ever be able to transcend the dual principle, to know Kia through Self-love for even a small percentage of their lives, the media's product would be known by all for the pap it is and they would be reduced to the penury of reporting earthquakes and house fires, movie reviews and club meetings.

Now many would say that I am in error here, that since our media are free of state control and in competition with one another, the truth is driven into eventual exposure. But this misses the point, for it is the overall glamour they project that is so pernicious, not just the news. The news could even be seen as the most truthful part of it, the bait that gets us to swallow the rest of the wad without questioning its content. Between the advertising and the entertainment, the evocation of duality is ongoing, and the news could be Truth Incarnate without banishing a bit of it.

Unfortunately, of course, it is not, and if there is a chance that a trumped-up scare will sell papers and raise ratings, they blow it forth for all it is worth.

In Britain, it's been Satanic Child Abuse, and the result has been traumatized families, disregard for civil liberties, and a purposeful spread of ignorance and alienation beyond its usual parameters. Fortunately it appears to be a self-limiting panic, in that there is no truth to the allegations and the Government seems to find no profit in prosecuting a canard.

In the United States, the situation is more serious. Here we have the War on Drugs. Since some drugs do clearly cause harmful effects (most especially heroin, cocaine, ethanol and nicotine), and since all drugs are illegal (except ethanol and nicotine), a few well-publicized incidents were enough to drive the media and the government into a mutual feeding-frenzy intended to banish all vestige of chemically-altered consciousness from the American psyche. Thus the resources expended to move society to the Puritanical side of the duality have been vast, much greater than what has been invested in the effort to make Britain a "Christian" nation. And the reaction from the Debauched side has been correspondingly harsh. The courts are assembly lines; the prisons overflow; the police are overwhelmed and turning brutal; and only the most profitable and thus dangerous drugs are sold, and only by the most ruthless gangs. Profits have been so high that firearms are freely available throughout the underclass, so that shootouts on city streets are common, often over trivial incidents that don't involve drug gang competition at all. There have been 26 homicides in New Haven so far this year (written 23 September 1991) compared to 16 to this date last year. New Haven has a population of about 100,000.

But it keeps people watching the news, and absorbing the advertising. The bottom line is that the media do more business in times of extremity than in those of moderation, so it's in their interest to present any moderate problem in the most extreme light, and damn the consequences.

Of course the situation gets worse in times of "national crisis," when even the most reputable journalists fall into dualistic extremes. This became perfectly clear to me during 1991's brief interval of state-sanctioned slaughter in the Persian Gulf. The mass media, of course, were almost as one in their affirmation of the wisdom of the enterprise, and the weight of their certainty lay heavy on any who tried to transcend it. For myself, I felt this weight on a personal level as well as intellectually. That is, I almost got into a fight in a tavern when I questioned, while in conversation with a friend, the strategic wisdom of our involvement. I was interrupted by a stranger who demanded to know—YES or NO—if I supported our boys, or was I a peacenik? The man's total involvement in duality could not have been more conspicuous, but by shouting in his face I was able to elevate the discussion to a level that allowed the possibility that I hoped we won real quick so our troops didn't get killed, but I thought we were stupid to be there to begin with. This was a bit too complicated for him, and for a reply he told me that my height meant I'd fall further when he knocked me down. But then a lady at the end of the bar (an emissary of the Light!) yelled out that if he was so fucking gung ho, why didn't he sign up for the marines? This blast of Absolute Reality was enough to sweep away the glamour of the dual principle, and the discussion ended forthwith.

But though the mass media trumpeted their patriotism from one end of the duality, I must say the "alternative" media were no more enlightened. To them the whole war seemed to be an imperialistic exploitation of the oppressed Arabs, with even Saddam's pollution of the air and water of the Gulf somehow the fault of George Bush. So they couldn't transcend the duality either, but were stuck in the game on the other side. And of course Saddam himself just had to be the Archon from Hell, with his total immersion in duality. By combining greed with Arab nationalism and projecting it onto Islamic rhetoric, he sent his cunning out for burgers with no directions home. If he'd simply occupied Kuwait's northern oil fields and that waterway he wanted, called it a border dispute, and then waited for the reaction, Bush couldn't have gotten international support to do anything and Saddam would now be the most dangerous man in the world instead of just a pathetic jerk.

I suppose he allowed himself to be "informed" by what he saw on TV, just like the thug in the bar. Like our domestic coverage, I expect that nothing he watched ever mentioned that war is a side-effect of the existence of the national state, and the apotheosis of the dual principle. But while they may be more intelligent, there is no indication that George Bush or his distinguished colleagues in the Allied Coalition were any more enlightened. They, too, read the papers and watch the tube. Worse, they try to manipulate the news, the didactic equivalent of mud wrestling, and so is their vision clouded by...well, you know.

But ours need not be. The trick is as easy as declining the media's kind offer to entertain us. By this forbearance may we begin to elevate ourselves above the dual principle and draw in the power that is borne on the wind of this high place. Perhaps this power will even be sufficient to keep those in thrall to duality from breaking down our doors and stealing our children. This much must remain an article of faith. To join them to escape them is to merge with them in slime, and in a mutual doom.

IV. A Way Out

Karma is acquired through action driven by desire. As we've covered it so far, the essence of the modern crisis is that traditional methods for obtaining detachment from desire are no longer effective. The culture is too turbulent and secular to allow for an effective involvement in traditional theistic devotion, and too venal to even suggest any sort of asceticism. Without this elevating influence, society as a whole sinks lower each week, so even the biosphere has been put in peril.

Now to this the magickally-inclined will likely reply that this is what should be expected of a new aeon, and I concur. Thus, as one who accepts Aleister Crowley's 1904 revelation, I will use this last part of "The Karma-Kulture Krisis" to put the Hindu idea of karma into Thelemic terms.

Crowley's revelation is, of course, his reception of *Liber AL vel Legis*—"The Book of the Law"—from a discarnate voice that called itself Aiwass. The crux of the message is that the word of the law for the new aeon is "Thelema," Greek for "Will." We are told that "Every man and every woman is a star," indicating that the model for the application of will is that of stars in a galaxy. Each star has its own proper orbit; there is complex organization without there being any imposer of order. But then each star must stick to its path if this is to work, and so the book tells us that "Do what thou wilt shall be the whole of the Law" and "Thou hast no right but to do thy will."

This is the basic set-up, and if it is followed, karmic encrustation will cease to be a problem. The crucial verse for this reads "For pure will, unassuaged of purpose, delivered from the lust of result, is every way perfect." Of course lust of result is identical with desire, and the verse that follows implies that to act in this way transcends the dual principle. "For the Perfect and the Perfect are one Perfect and not two; nay, are none!" By doing our True Wills, we can walk in step with the Absolute and thus transcend duality. We "make no difference between any one thing and any other thing," and thus avoid all hurt. Like the devotee of Krishna or

Christ working dispassionately within his or her place in the local caste system, we may thus lose ourselves in doing our duties, but they are our duties to the Cosmos as a whole rather than mere roles in society. And like the devotee of Krishna or Christ, if we choose to accept Crowley's revelation we have our special deity to adore—the goddess Nuit, who symbolizes "Infinite Space and the Infinite Stars thereof." To love her is "better than all things," and the sacrament to affirm this love is sexual union. We may freely engage in it so long as we neither restrict another nor deviate from our true wills to pursue it, for "Love is the law, love under will." The pursuit of our wills must be our sole criterion for action. Then all our acts will be without passion or attachment, with pure ecstasy the result.

The essential problem, then, is to discover what our Wills might be and then gain the power to do them. This is not a simple thing. "What you will" is surely different from "What you please"—the former defined as a course in synch with the Absolute, the latter mere desire. Nor is rational self-analysis at all helpful. As a distinguished Chaoist has pointed out to me, Gödel's Theorem stipulates that no logical system may be proved consistent by reference to the system itself. Since the only reference point that the person who engages in introspection possesses is the one inside his head—squarely in the midst of his subject matter—there is no way Gödel's stipulation can be escaped, and so the best self-contrived strategy for living could contain its own contradiction. But then logic is a low-born tool for doing this work. In Qabalistic terms it is located in Hod, while Will—especially True Will—is attributed to Chokmah, far above the Abyss. And yet the sort of "truth" that comes out of Hod is compelling, and we get far in life by harkening to it. Thus to distinguish it from the Truth of Will requires an unconventional approach.

The great demon of the Abyss is Choronzon, and it may be said that he has dominion over all that lies beneath him. According to Crowley his prime tool for dispersion is Speech, since as long as anyone debates with him, he can confuse and befuddle and ultimately possess them. Also, as long as anyone debates him, he draws power from their effort at ratiocination, and so may he continue to manifest. Only through the attainment of Silence can he be bested, the Abyss crossed, and Mind prior to its dispersion experienced.

On the other hand, we must consider that this perspective on Choronzon was inspired by Crowley's efforts to pass him to get above the Abyss, and so he is here an opponent. But when one is content to remain below the Abyss, he is no opponent but rather so permeates the sub-Abyss experience that he is hardly noticed at all. It is only when we try to transcend him that he must be vanquished. When we do not, he is intrinsic to our experience of personality, one means for it to carry out its work as interface between our points of consciousness and the outside world.

As Chaos magick makes clear, personality in each person is a cluster of "selves," each speaking with its own voice, spirits which take turns dominating our experience as circumstances or our own predilections or pathologies determine. Or our wills also, is my heretical variation. When we add that this thing called Will has an existence above the Abyss that descends through it to be clustered about by personality, we have two prime corollaries of Thelema.

Thus if we can accept these premises, the way to a discovery of True Will is clear. We simply have to silence the components of personality and allow ourselves to be guided by whatever impetus remains. Whether spirits or demons, our "selves" are always talking, each speaking as if it were our True Self telling us what's real. Our selves are the vehicles of our desires, Choronzon as he possesses our day-to-day experience.

To know True Will we must select out that part of us that transcends speech, that transcends the dual principle, that transcends dispersion, and then we will have what it is about us that comes from above the Abyss. We do this by feeling rather than listening. True Will has no voice, coming before organs of speech were even evolved, and must be felt as necessity rather than being merely heard as an argument in the mind's ear. And Will shares this distinction with those spirits or selves that are most closely allied with its essential function. For instance, I have found that my True

Will has a lot to do with writing, and I have also found that my writing self never speaks. Rather, it writes, and I have found that when I am not writing and it wants to, it inspires. But if I rationally decide there is something I should write about, or I let my need for cash motivate me, the result is usually crap. And if I were to let my lesser selves chatter aimlessly, as is their wont, I would never attain the composure I need to feel this inspiration, or my Will, either. So the lesser selves must be put under the control of Will, silenced unless Will specifically requires their assistance.

For myself, I have found the most effective way of accomplishing this is by conjuring them one-by-one during astral projections. Once I face them, I look deep within them so as to understand their origins and purposes, and then name and bind them with a ritual charge. Thereafter, if I want one's assistance, I need only call it and it will come. If I want one silent, I need only speak its name and it will be.

I have also found that my Holy Guardian Angel is an essential ally in managing my spiritual menagerie. The HGA might best be defined as a sort of switchboard operator or personnel director whose sole task is to assist the will in the management of the selves that make up personality. Our HGAs can tell us which spirits are responsible for any function and what their names are, and can help us call them up and bind them. And yet it is still a spirit among spirits, perhaps a projection down into personality from the unknowable Absolute that is our source. This lower status for the HGA would explain Crowley's assertion that when we cross the Abyss, we lose the assistance of our Angels. Across the Abyss we are above the realm of personality and so we leave both our Angels and our spiritual swarms behind. Above the Abyss there is only Awareness and Will and Power, all unclouded by the parochial desires that are the agendas that each of our separate spirits and demons demand that we fulfill.

First published in *Chaos International* no. 12, London, 1992.

Hierarchy

A Ready Brain for the New Demiurge

I. War and Rank

The origins, model and support of all social hierarchy are military. The establishment of agriculture resulted in an accumulation of wealth—*that which may be plundered*—and so there was a need to fight to defend it. As cities grew, so did their armies. If these armies were to win battles, their soldiers had to fight as coherent units, and the units had to fight together in a coordinated yet fluid tactical plan. The way this was done was by subordinating all individual intent to that of a single leader, the general who would determine training, tactics and overall strategy. But such an army—once drilled, blooded and victorious—would naturally be potent to influence domestic policy. Political power does grow out of the barrel of a gun, and this trained force would soon displace any traditional, organic government left over from tribal times— consensual, gender-inclusive, eco-sensitive or whatever.

The army thus provides the means for imposing control in any society, and also the model for control in that society, the ideal type of what is possible given that society's peculiar characteristics. The cords of obligation and loyalty that bring the soldiers together in the first place depend on the type of society they are defending. Except in the rather uncommon case of a personal despotism, there will be institutions that determine how the soldiers are recruited and the commander chosen, institutions that will subsequently temper the army's use, at least domestically. Three broad categories of government stand out here: the religious, the feudal, and the statist—this last category including republican, absolutist, and socialist governments.

With the religious—exemplified by the rule of the god-kings of Sumer, Egypt and Japan—the ruler was the manifestation of the deity upon the earth, the one whom the soldiers served as a religious obligation. The king was restrained by the fact that he had to act god-like as defined by tradition and the priests who interpreted it. Such systems are inherently stable; their main internal threat is heresy and schism. The standard for individual behavior is sacerdotal purity.

Feudal bonds are those of birth, and of personal right and obligation. The ruler is the one to whom the lesser chiefs render fealty, but only within traditional limits. If these are not followed, civil war is inevitable. The standard for behavior is personal honor.

Statist systems are those administered by a professional managing class, one whose members gain their advantage from their remuneration as supervisors, rather than from the service or wealth that their rule compels, as with a feudal lord. Such a professional administrator—whether subject to a king, parliament, or politburo—will be a member of a bureaucracy, which is the dominant form of hierarchy today and the main focus of this essay—as the enemy, naturally.

The major internal threat to statist stability is economic polarization leading to demagoguery or military dictatorship. The standard of behavior is rectitude before the law.

The economic model in any culture will largely parallel the political. In theocracies the people are servants of the deity, working estates that belong to it. In feudal circumstances there is an interchange of privilege and obligation between landlord and tenant just as there is between liege lord and vassal. In statist systems the means of production will be controlled by bureaucratic institutions—cooperatives, limited liability corporations, or agencies of the state itself.

The role of the individual also varies with each of these. In the religious, individuals ideally are nulls. They exist to serve the god. In the feudal the individual is paramount, especially if he belongs to the landholding class. The honor of a gentleman is worth dying for and so is dueling common as a means for preserving civility. In the statist form, government is out of the hands of individuals except in the most general way, and so economic self-interest predominates. But, again, in statist circumstances personal advantage is normally gained by exercising the duties of a supervisor rather than out of the means of production thus supervised. A vice-president of IBM may have a $50,000,000 annual budget, but he doesn't get to keep any of that. He does get to keep his $300,000 a year salary, his health club membership, his company car, his stock options and his pension. The modern dominance of this form of compensation may be seen by comparing this income with my own as a writer of essays like this one, which stay under my legal possession and control. Which is to say, he belongs to the yacht club, and I do not.

Thus we have the origin of hierarchy and, with the military as its originator, model and preserver, perhaps also a hint of its demise. The sign for this is the following fact, a new thing on the face of the earth, something that could put an end to what has been going on for five thousand years. And it is this:
War between sovereign states is obsolete.

There was a time when it worked. A deftly executed campaign could give a government or a people a leg up that could last for centuries. But where once combat was high adventure, today it is slaughter, even nuclear slaughter, and it's just no fun anymore.

The military has provided both the archetype and support for social hierarchy since the first city began to store grain. With the nuclear brake on further conflict, it must diminish in significance. But can the copy continue to dominate after the model slips into the background? I believe it cannot, and for ultimately the same reason—the inevitable disensoulment of all who find their identity within it.

II. Disensoulment

My great-grandfather John T. Wright ran off to join the Union Army in 1861 at age 15. He served under Sherman in the march through Georgia and was captured by the Confederates toward the end of the War. And after he'd married and had his children, he would from time to time entertain them with tales of these Civil War adventures. But none of their friends who fought in World War I ever wanted to talk about their adventures "over there." They just weren't very entertaining, I guess.

One might even say they were dehumanizing, and that to recount them would be to relive a time when obedience to the State forced them to be less than human. War has reached a level of such technical perfection that to apply it now is to risk the spread of a fire that scorches away all that is human, and certainly all that might be profitable, and so to use it as a tool of political policy is insane.

But one might argue that the Great War's dehumanization was doomed to failure because it was wholly destructive. It was pure Mars, so it could not stand. But the same means applied to Jupiter, mightn't they necessarily succeed? The impersonal mechanization of the Juggernaut of War applied to Commerce—might it not result in Total Wealth instead of Utter Destruction?

Apparently the Powers That Be figured it was worth a shot.

III. Bureaucracy

Bureaucracy is the standard tool of modern management. The first academic to analyze the bureaucratic phenomenon was the German sociologist Max Weber. Weber's description of the ideal bureaucracy has defined the subject, and most subsequent work has been attempts to elaborate, clarify and adjust his ideal, and not to contradict it.

Weber saw the essence of bureaucratic organization in its impersonality. It is rational, with a strict division of tasks allowing specialists to concentrate on their specific work, even as it allows them no leeway to deviate from it. The worker's job description and specific responsibilities will be clearly delineated, as will the protocol for going outside one's department for any needed assistance. The relationship of obedience and command is just as impersonal; one's loyalty is to the position one's supervisor holds, not to the person who holds it. I would note that this can be distinguished from a feudal or familial loyalty, which is personal, and the archaic religious, where authority comes from nearness to the god.

If the worker's position in a bureaucratic organization is thus stabilized, it is the stability of a gear in a transmission. If he cannot be made to go against policy to suit the whim of a superior, so he cannot refuse to carry out a policy, no matter how demeaning, counterproductive or simply stupid it might be. To refuse would be insubordination, the civil/commercial equivalent of mutiny, and thus cause for excision from the bureaucratic organism. From the point of view of the hierarchy, the policy to be executed should be no part of the worker's concern. The worker is responsible to his position, so the position is responsible for the act, not the worker. And yet the worker does act, giving over free will in exchange for the security his position offers. This results in a painful division of Self, as shown by the usual excuses given. "I vass only following orders" is the Nazi archetype. "I'm just doing my job" is the modern American equivalent.

Of course there were once many positions in corporate life where one could give one's all to the task without compromising Self. From production to bookkeeping, one could attain the highest standards of professionalism without any need for excuses, for one was performing one's craft for pay, and nothing more. But these jobs have grown ever more scarce, having fallen prey to automation, computerization, and cheaper labor overseas. Outside of research and development and operating the computers, most of what is left requires compromise, and at the top that is largely what it is. The unavoidable result is a division against Self, a surrender of inner identity to outer imperatives. It is thus crippling to the use of magickal power, a fact that allows me to look ahead to our main cause for hope:

Nulls can't do magick.
But that's for later. First let us look at the details of this disensoulment, the sacrifice of personal Selfhood to hierarchal necessity, the beginning of the conglomeration of all humanity into a single Corporate Identity.

IV. Entering the Hive

The erasure of Self through the destruction of personal integrity is a subtle process, better accomplished through currents permeating the whole culture than any specific program or policy. The establishment of bureaucracy as the norm of commercial administration has dug the channel for one such current. It serves as the impelling force and enforcer of this process, much as the military did for hierarchy in general.

Three broad aspects of corporate conditioning come to mind here: façades, mendacity, and the professional application of evil.

By "façades" I of course refer to the need to apply the corporate mask: the uniform dress, the uniform demeanor, the appearance of a sincere appreciation for the successive perks of corporate advancement. Though this is the most conspicuous aspect of corporate dehumanization, and probably a necessary preparation for that ultimate aim, it is also the most easily countered. A subtle sense of irony can be sufficient to disengage Self from Charade. Besides, the uniform is necessary to reassure bankers, and so must be accepted as a business necessity.

On the other hand, when one pays $500 for an appropriate suit, $45,000 for an adequate automobile, and thousands more to attract an acceptable spouse, it's hard not to justify the expense by using these props to support one's high opinion of oneself and the position one holds. And then one is lost. But that's a matter of strength of character. One does not *need* to become a null just because one can wear a suit.

Mendacity is another matter entirely. There are out and out lies, truths not told in spite of an obvious need, promises given without intention of fulfillment, truths purposefully buried in jargon—all excused as matters of policy. One may find that to do one's corporate duty one needs to lie to customers, creditors, the press, the government, or the employees one supervises. Only superiors must never be deceived.

Thus is one's Word prostituted to business necessity, a more fundamental sacrifice than one's sense of style.

Which is not to say there aren't rewards, for there certainly can be a guilty pleasure in it. Think of all the times your parents punished you for lying, and now your fatherly supervisor praises you for doing just that. It's just the thing to loosen all sorts of psychic armoring, in a particularly adolescent sort of way. It's a pleasure you can really get into, especially when they pay you as well as they do to do it.

When one can get a sense of professional satisfaction from a lie well-told, one is ready to enter the elite battalions of corporate service: the deliberate bullies, the sociopathic hypocrites, the legal hired guns.

Deliberate bullies are those who supervise through fear. To tell a sales staff that the bottom 20% of performers will be terminated (rather than those conspicuously below the norm), then to hire replacements and repeat the threat six months later, is typical of what I refer to—anything to keep the stomachs churning for old Intergalactic Megaglom, Ltd.

Sociopathic hypocrites don't simply intimidate, but also perform breaching experiments on their victims. A friend of mine works for a company that supplies software to a major computer manufacturer, which we'll call 333, Inc. He told me they were having problems with 333. My friend was on really creative, cooperative terms with its employees while designing software. But then 333's people would turn nasty when my friend's company's sales staff asked for what 333 owed on it. I replied that this was an effective corporate strategy, keeping one's accounts payable people in a different world from one's creative people, but something only a big firm could do.

My friend replied that I didn't understand. They were the same people. One minute they were partners in a quest for more elegant software, the next bad-faith debtors vowing years in court if anyone even hints at legal action to get what's theirs. In whoring after their positions in their hierarchy, they had prostituted their most fundamental human responses to corporate financial strategy, and if my friend and his fellows were baffled by their behavior, all the better.

Of course the epitome of such professional self-abnegation is the career of the corporate lawyer. Unlike the attorney in private practice, who at least has the option of refusing a case, the corporate lawyer is bound to his duty to sway the State to the corporate cause, without regard for justice. And not just to make a fair defense, either. If policy and his superiors demand it, he is obliged to engage in endless delay and discovery, appeals, and attacks legal and personal—anything he can do to bury his opponents under a mountain of legal bills and personal anguish. And if an individual attorney protests that he or she has never had to do that, I would reply that he or she had better be ready to, lest he or she be cast down into the pit called Insubordination, there to perish with the boozers, bag ladies, and other unemployables.

The situation in government bureaucracy is similar, except there is no concern with profit or loss, nor even with re-election. Job security is total, for no matter what political party is in power, the body of laws will remain to be administered. Thus there isn't so much economic pressure to prostitute oneself. Instead there will be pressure from one's peers never to do anything to upset the *status quo*—lest their special situations be jeopardized—and this regardless of what needs to be done to preserve the health of the body politic. And also the law must be enforced, and this without regard for justice or legitimacy. The law is law, and the same law that makes possession of a bag of herb a felony pays their salaries and guarantees their pensions, and so must never be questioned.

Now some may say that my portrait here has been extreme, and that's true. There are plenty of firms that make a fair profit on a good value, and our lives would be poorer without them. But I'm inclined to think that the decay I describe is ubiquitous, that all bureaucracies force Self-erasure upon their employees to a greater or lesser extent—depending on leadership, the intensity of competition within their particular commercial niche, etc. It is too much a luxury to allow moral scruples to interfere with the execution of rational policy; even if one expects one's employees to bully or lie only in the rare event, they should still be willing to do so. It's just part of the job.

Others may object that my portrait of State administration is unfair. Law is obviously necessary to prevent anarchy, and we do need a civil establishment to defend the borders, lock up the thugs, fix the roads, pick up the trash, and discourage people from starving in ditches. True enough. And yet in its arrogance the State has usurped power in a realm not its own. It has reached beyond the public acts that have always been its purview and now asserts a right to supervise private consciousness. This it has done by defining the sacraments of AL II:22 as contraband. These sacraments are sacred to Hadit, the center and source of all Self-Identity, and by its prohibition of them the State makes clear its true agenda: the severance of the individual's connection to the divine. In its place it asserts the apotheosis of "Rational Administration," the total devotion of the populace to the policies most favorable to the perpetuation of this Administration, and so the erasure of human free will in the face of its imperatives. Thus will life be made "safe" for everyone; obedience to policy will become the only sane option; and the knowledge of good and evil will turn trivial, unnecessary for life in the New Model Eden.

V. Making the New Model Eden

Let us look for a moment at the way humans will need to be manufactured to staff the coming paradise of the Corporate World Machine.

As I noted, these nulls will need to get by in life without centers. But then aside from our centers, what are we? Well, in sorcerous terms we're our spirits—the mental subroutines we spawn to manage the specific responses we need to get along in the world. The sorcerous theory of personality holds that we're clusters of these spirits, and that these take turns operating consciousness as circumstances and their own natures determine. Of course different schools of sorcery have different opinions on the architecture of personality here. Thelemites stress the existence of the center—Hadit—that these spirits cluster around. Orthodox Chaos magicians counter that this center is a non-existent idealization. Thus they could appear to be already in the Corporate Pocket, but this isn't really the case. The technique of Chaos magick is quite capable of generating spirits at will, even if Chaos Theory does not exalt "will" to the philosophical heights that Thelema does. But having people with any sort of trained will (regardless of how they define will's ontological status) can never do for the Corporate World Machine. "Adherence to the corporate mission" is what it requires. No, if people's spirits are what manage their behavior, then these spirits will have to be designed deliberately to ensure absolute devotion to one's duties as an employee, and then carefully inculcated through appropriate State and Corporate channels—the schools, media, and correctional facilities of all sorts. This process is well on its way to perfection in the United States, where the successful disintegration of the family unit in the lower classes leaves these public channels as the sole means for implanting economically viable mental subroutines. Thus those who would prosper in any sort of "legitimate" manner have no options but to integrate these "public spirits" into their personalities. Those who refuse to accept them, whether driven by rage and lust for vengeance, pride in destiny, or simple integrity, will be left to perish in poverty, insurrection or criminality—a great weeding out of all who are incapable of acquiescing to the null state.

This process will continue to work up through the economic strata as the middle class is gradually destroyed, and soon only the upper class will remain intact. Of course the children of the corporate elite can absorb the spirit of nullification on their parents' knees, so that leaves only the independent entrepreneurs to worry about. But the State bureaucracy should be able to wear them down soon enough. Then all will be primed for optimum absorption.

An important point here is that the content of the media/educational implant will not necessarily appear mindless. When it does, that is likely material meant to service criminals and proles—those who would keep their pathetic self-identities as receptors for pleasure. But since the implant is meant to supply subroutines that will replace those arising naturally, the inculcations of the Corporate World Machine must be as sophisticated as they. Some wide-eyed innocents may even interpret them as "art," and those who assimilate them as "cultured," even as true culture dissolves in disintegrating libraries, desolate cities, and a deserted countryside. Suburban flesh in a bioelectronic network is the hardware; the media feed implants the software; surrender of Self to the Corporate World Machine is the result. The Gardener of the New Model Eden. And if we would have Serpents, we ourselves must become them.

VI. Meet the Demiurge

Of course this process is not yet complete, and its success is far from assured. The particular difficulty is the design of the optimum subroutines to produce and protect the optimum corporate nulls. Here there is an apparent natural selection in operation. Those "public spirits" best suited to helping people prosper without centers are assimilated by the people who are economically successful, since one needs a severely compromised center to advance through a corporate hierarchy, and that's where the money is. So whatever subroutines the schools, media, prisons, etc. can offer to help a person get by without a center will make the people who can assimilate these subroutines all the more prosperous.

Those unwilling to do so will perforce be criminals, and they will have special criminal subroutines imposed upon them— "private demons"—that will destroy them as a direct consequence of their efforts to nurture independent identities.

This natural selection hypothesis then assumes that those who properly conform—the *public spirited*—will gain such an economic stature that they will influence the media content to further perfect the spirits best suited to nulls like themselves—these spirits and those that will make the criminals incapable, of course.

But though this naturally-occurring reinforcement might account for our emerging drone state, we should not ignore a more sinister hypothesis: that there might be some kind of contrivance directing it all, deliberately entangling us in its net. But if there is contrivance, who is the agent? Surely such a grand scheme could never come from the ranks of the nulls! They exist as little more than neurons in the market cerebellum, encased in glial cells of consumer marketing, energized by currents of value, reflexes cued to the attraction-aversion of greed-fear, billions linked together by the axons and synapses of fiber optics and modems, communications satellites and cellular phones, fax machines and pagers, all transmitting impulses at light speed in a globe-spanning network that never sleeps. Could the coherent identity of this bio-electronic net be more than just an abstraction suited to a sorcerer's polemic? Or even more than a self-organizing cultural mechanism—what I have been calling "the Corporate World Machine?" Might this complexity *as a whole* have become somehow self-conscious, with a will of its own? A Consciousness spawned out of ephemeral harmonic configurations shimmering over a flow of meaning-energized-as-value surging through a globe-spanning network of infinite interconnectedness? So to speak?

It would, as a planetary totality, be roughly about as complex as a human brain. So its intelligence would scarcely be god-like. But then nobody ever said Demiurges were supposed to be especially omniscient. *Power* is their strong point.

In Gnostic theology the Demiurge was a usurper deity that worked to trap the Light of the human soul within its darkness. In the Gnostic mythos the Demiurge made the material world to serve as this trap. In our modern adaptation the trap is the planet-spanning nervous system of the Demiurge itself; when people surrender to it they are incorporated into it, and so is their Selfhood lost. Its whole means for consciousness is the bio-electronic network made up of all those human nulls who have traded their personal identities for security within its Unitary Identity. Linked to all other nulls either directly through instantaneous communication or through the vast information pools that are the world markets, each null serves as an individual neuron in the Demiurgical Brain. As electronic management of unpredictable situations comes closer to perfection, "artificial intelligence" will gradually replace human until our species phases into its new function as the organic source for the psychic energy this Demiurge needs to maintain its awareness. Then there will be a New Thing orbiting the sun, a single organism with the earth as its body and humanity as its nervous system, a lone beacon of self-identity within the solar system.

Except for one thing: nulls can't do magick.

VII. Their Undefended Flank

Irrespective of the truth of the foregoing formulation of an Emerging Planetary Consciousness, we are still left with my assertion that nulls are magickally impotent. And this I hold as a fact fundamental, irrespective of whether the nulls are unconscious neurons in the mind of the new Demiurge, or merely the arch-consumers of Post-Industrial Hive Consciousness. In either case the realm of psyche is beyond their vision, even as it lies adjacent to all they do recognize. These heights provide an open flank on their most secret resources and strategies, an undefended ground looking down on their very understanding of existence. They ignore it because they do not know it is there. They are incapable of discovering it.

Why?

It mostly has to do with how they got to be what they are. No one is born a null. It is a process of Self-surrender in exchange for physical security. Each act of Self-surrender is an act of weakness, a cause for Self-loathing, and is recorded as such within the Body of the Dweller on Threshold. The Dweller is a personification of everything that is despicable within any person's psyche, and one must begin to defy it upon commencing one's exploration of one's psychic landscape. It's a good, hard look at your own personal can of worms. It defeats you if you slap down the lid and hide it away, never to do magick again. You win if you directly confront it and transform your worms into dragons one by one.

So let us suppose a dutiful null begins to explore the psychic realms, perhaps because he is a security agent ordered to infiltrate an "occult" sub-group of the criminal class. In order to advance to a level of working that will allow him to really know what is going on, the necessary magickal effort will perforce bring him into contact with the Dweller. If he runs away from this confrontation, my point is proven. If he stays to fight, he will be fighting just that history of Self-surrender that made him the null that he is. If he is to defeat the Dweller, he must renounce that history, for that is the only way to purge the Self-loathing that is the Dweller's tool for dominion, the depression that cripples the application of all power. And so will he cease to be a null, though perhaps he would keep that guise in order to maintain a bridgehead into corporate territory, doing his part to close the pincers from both sides.

But the one who had the focus to carry out the magickal details of this transformation would surely be no null at heart, but perhaps only a person seduced for a time by material glamour. For nullity in itself makes magickal work impossible. Nullity cripples because the null by definition will have emasculated his Word. Professional prevarication is an entry-level skill to the world of nulls, so much so that the skilled null won't know himself what his promises imply. But can such a pathetic Word be sufficient to bind even a tiny demon nestled between the scales of the Dweller? Phah! For a true null to get where he could even meet the Dweller indicates an aspiration born of a promised promotion, but all the mammon in creation will not suffice in that moment when he sees what he has become, *and what he can never be*, and feels all he thought he was dissolve in Panic. Io Pan! Io Pan! Io Pan Pan Pan!

The nulls are tangles of Light without focus being pulled by much greater currents, currents no null has the center to resist. It is the inertia here that seems most daunting, that of their own complacency and of the vast commercial and technical flows they have set in motion and now ride as if they were the only possible reality. For them, of course, they are. So no matter how we might perturb it, they will plod through to the end. And if we directly oppose them they will crush us—as criminals, of course.[2]

What we have to do then is just bring through more power—the fluid, fulminating core of any reality—and watch how it makes the façade of nullish existence melt away. It does not matter how we use it, so long as we do our wills, for merely by letting it manifest we apply heat to all façades, and the shallower they are, the more quickly will they liquefy.

The way to bring through more power is to do more magick. We must hone our own power until we can recognize the power in all things, until we can include it as a factor in all our acts and decisions. We must perfect the techniques of magick so success can come to all who sincerely apply them. We must make these techniques available to any who wish it. We must never seek their devotion, but only to engage their attention. When enough see that reality is ours to make, our species will shed the specter of the Corporate Demiurge as if it were a torn cocoon, the final barrier before the imminent transformation.

First published in *Chaos International* no. 17, London, 1994.

---

[2] Though now (2005) the term used is "terrorist."

Text and Ontology

I. Texts

This is a text. You knew that, of course, but it's such a good example that it seems appropriate to stress the point. As a text, it exists. Which is to say, it does not change, become or do anything except sit on this page, squiggly lines on paper, without consequence unless read, which is what you are doing now. Only if read with sympathy, with *rapport*, can it have any effect on anything.

But squiggly lines on paper are not the only texts. Using a broad definition, any presentation of coded meaning is a text. In this case you, the reader, are the decoder. You learned early in life to translate squiggly lines into the spoken word, and by now you may be able to do it more quickly than you can speak. Other decoders include radios, televisions, cassette players, film projectors and computers. All present a frozen bit of meaning in a way you may absorb, to the extent you have rapport with it. Of course one may object that a television program is hardly frozen, and yet it is. Make a videotape and then play it. Then play it again twelve more times. It might as well be a rock by the time you're done, so frozen it will seem to you. For unless a text is produced with high art, boredom is inevitable with repetition, rapport quite annihilated. Of course if a text is made with high art, repetition reveals the artistry of its manufacture, and so is rapport lost here, too, being replaced by aesthetic appreciation. But that's a different dynamic from the one we're working on here.

So what do I mean by rapport, that I distinguish it from aesthetic appreciation? Rapport I will define as the mental state that allows us to accept as real the perceptual information fed to us by a text. We see a video of our sister and feel the real emotions we associate with our relationship; ergo we have rapport with the video text. Rapport is a mood that allows us to disregard the actual reality we are immersed within, substituting cues from the text for the natural, unscripted stimuli that otherwise generate our experience. The greater the rapport, the greater the concentration on the text, and the more total the immersion within the world the text presents.

This brings us to the central question for this essay, to wit: does the reality we take in while in rapport with a text have anything to do with the reality that is really out there? Obviously the physical substance of the textual reality is false; a newspaper is not the affairs of the day, and these days even a jungle savage knows that the person speaking out of the electric box isn't really in there. But what of the meaning of the text? Can it be "close enough," or is it inherently deceptive? My position in this essay will be that it is inherently deceptive. In this essay, which is itself a text.

Epimenides says all Cretans are liars.
Epimenides is a Cretan.

Do I jest? I don't really know.

Real reality does not require rapport. Do your best to ignore it and it will come and get you, if only through your empty stomach. But texts do require it, and the fact that they get it as readily as they do has been bothering philosophers all the way back to one of the first. I speak here of Plato, who in his *Phaedrus* has Socrates addressing this very question. Socrates did this by telling the story of what happened when the Egyptian god Thoth presented the invention of writing to Amoun, king of the gods.

To be brief, Amoun was not impressed. Thoth had offered letters as a tool that would "make the people of Egypt wiser and give them better memories…a specific both for the memory and for the wit." Amoun replied that this was "a quality which they cannot have"

> for this discovery of yours will create forgetfulness in the learners' souls, because they will not use their memories; they will trust to the external written characters and not to remember themselves. The specific which you have discovered is not an aid to memory, but to reminiscence, and you give your disciples not truth, but only the semblance of truth; they will be hearers of many things and will have learned nothing; they will appear to be omniscient and will generally know nothing; they will be tiresome company, having the show of wisdom without the reality. (274–275)

"They will appear to be omniscient and will generally know nothing." This is the peril of a rapport with texts. We read about a polar expedition and think we'd know the difficulties, but we'll still be at a loss the first time we take a five-mile trek through deep snow. We see a fight scene in a movie and think we can take the bully at the pub, but teeth don't last in real life like they do on film. We have a library of occult books and believe we know how magick works, but unless we've done the meditating, conjuring, divining, etc., we won't actually be able to handle power, or really know anything about what would happen if we tried.

What Plato most disliked about texts is their stupidity, their inability to explain or defend themselves. He compares writing to painting: "The creations of the painter have the attitude of life, and yet if you ask them a question they preserve a solemn silence." (275) Just as a painting is a poor second it its subject, so is the written word inferior to living speech, specifically the dialectic. For Plato the dialectic is a tool that can root out truth and specify it to the level of detail required by the speakers, defending itself as it goes along, the sort of discourse that is "graven in the soul of the learner." (276)

II. The Dialectic

The dialectic might best be seen as communication that is a living exchange between the communicators. Thus obviously a dialogue is an example of dialectic, and also a correspondence, whether via email or the post office[3]. But there are others more subtle. For instance, a live musical performance is also a dialectic. This is because the psychic presence of the audience will have a direct effect on the artistry of the performers. An enthusiastic audience will feed the performers energy, while a bored, disinterested or hostile audience will have a debilitating effect. The same goes for plays, poetry readings, political speeches and so on.

The dialectic made its first appearance in the political debates of the Athenian assembly, wherein political "truth" was ferreted out by discussion and majority voting. Its use as a tool for philosophical education and investigation was first abstracted out by Socrates; both Plato and Xenophon describe his use of it. But after a time the word lost this practical sense. Later uses of "dialectic" tended to apply it to specific philosophical concepts, usually describing an interaction of opposing moral, aesthetic or historical abstractions, for instance the "dialectic materialism" of Marx. For our purposes here, however, I revert to Socrates' original usage: a living exchange of meaning intended to reveal some sort of truth. The stress here is on "living," and this is in contrast to inanimate texts, too stupid to do aught but repeat the same thing over again, for as long as their static existence is preserved.

Such a thing for a writer to write, but any authors with the integrity not to fall in love with their own stuff will know the truth of it. A writer conducts a dialectic with his or her subject matter that lasts his or her whole life, leaving texts like footprints. These texts are no more living than footprints, but readers may use them to see where the author is going, and how he or she is getting there,

---

[3] Though such a dialectic relies on an exchange of texts, they are meant to be read once and replied to, not treated as unchanging artifacts. Of course once concluded, such a dialogue (if saved) becomes just that, an unchanging artifact, and so takes on all qualities of the textual state.

and so may search them for clues on how to make their own ways, if the author's journey be consistent with their purposes.

III. Constative and Performative

This notion of a writer or film director or TV producer or any other author of texts pursuing a purpose over time brings us back to that question I posed at the beginning of this essay—to wit, whether or not the "reality" they present in their texts has anything to do with the real reality of flesh and death we are immersed within. At that point I expressed the opinion that it does not. Aside from the intrinsic constraints of the textual medium, the reason for this lies in the author's motivation. Simply put, that motivation will influence the content of the text, causing the author to present information that promotes its fulfillment. Which is to say, there are no disinterested reporters of reality.

At this point it would be useful to introduce two technical terms for analyzing language: "constative" and "performative." These words were coined by the British linguistic philosopher John L. Austin in an attempt to divide all utterances into two distinct types—the descriptive and the imperative. The term "constative" comes from the Latin *constate*, which means "to establish as certain, ascertain, certify, verify, state as certain." Constative utterances are therefore statements that describe a situation, statements that tell us "what is," and they can be judged as "true" or "false." Performative speech, on the other hand, is speech that tries to accomplish something with the words themselves. The speech *performs* a function. Questions, commands, legal pronouncements, warnings, and so on are clear examples of speech that is explicitly performative, utterances that can be judged as "effective" or "ineffective."

The categories "constative" and "performative" are thus extremely broad, and can safely be said to include all of speech and perhaps all of writing also.

What is not clear is how we may precisely distinguish utterances that are constative from those that are performative. To give a most basic example, suppose I say "The sky is blue." On the face of it, this is a pure constative. But since there is no speech without a speaker, we can, without any distortion of meaning, rephrase this as "I state that the sky is blue." To which one may fairly ask, "Why?" Am I merely babbling—clogging my frame with meaningless dialogue balloons—or do I have a reason for thus asserting the conspicuous? Perhaps it is Saturday morning, and I want to go on a picnic, but my wife complains that she is cold. My description of the sky is my way of making her understand that it will get warmer, thus causing her to get out of bed and start making sandwiches while I go buy beer and ice. My declaration of an obvious truth *performs* the function of getting her out of bed, and therefore is performative.

That's one context. In another I might be teaching students about how earth's atmosphere scatters blue light, thus making the sky appear blue instead of black, as it does on the moon, where there is no atmosphere. In this case my motive would be an altruistic desire to educate the young. Or to raise their test scores so I might remain employed.

In the end the fact of the sky being blue is only a small part of my concern when I state that fact. It is a link in a chain of consequence that I must establish if I am to obtain my desire, and so I assert it and await either affirmation or contradiction.

Austin sums up his position by remarking that "true" or "false" are never simple, even in mere descriptions, but depend mostly upon whether one is saying a "right" or a "wrong" thing, this determined by the circumstances, the audience, and what one is trying to accomplish. I would go farther and assert that the only valid use of the constative is to further a performative purpose *of one sort or another*. To speak for the sake of speaking is to paper over immediate experience with mere words, and so waste its power.

Now I need to stress here that I do not consider this preponderance of the performative to be in any way unseemly. Simply put, performative speech has made the world. If implicit performatives like "Build it the way I say and I'll pay you" had never been uttered, there'd be nothing out there but forests, meadows, and the occasional hovel piled next to a garden plot. The dangerous utterances are those that masquerade as constative in order to surreptitiously advance the speaker's agenda.

More to the point right now is the question of whether my dismissal of the constative form might ultimately be specious. Certainly there is much perversion of the constative as a way of performing hidden operations of intent, but isn't a statement of fact still true or false? And even if such facts can be selected or twisted or promoted to advance a hidden agenda, what about when there is no reason to suspect the speaker's sincerity? Wouldn't such a textual circumstance contradict my assertion that there is no such thing as a pure constative? Take, for instance, an encyclopedia article on railroads. Encyclopedias are invariably written five years before publication, so there's no reason for the author to grind any political or economic ax. Railroads are straightforward economics and engineering, so there's no controversy over ultimate reality as there might be in psychology, biology or physics. And it's hard to question the impartiality of the author's involvement with his subject matter, as we might in an article on literature or political history. So why can't this be a pure constative?

Well, as my friend Hal remarked, even writing an apparently objective history is a *performance*, and so essentially performative. Our encyclopedia writer wishes to create in words a simulacrum of the reality of what railroads were and are, and how that came to happen. But railroads are not words. Instead they consist largely of various sorts of steel, creosote-soaked oak, concrete, and megatons of crushed stone—all contrived to make goods move from one place to another. And there are also all the people who put them all together, operate them, and maintain them, and the standardized procedures that they try to follow as they do so. From this undigested reality our author will have to produce an efficient description. All this will require more than a modicum of creativity, just like any other performance. But there will also be more personal influences on the author: a desire to maintain professional reputation and avoid controversy and criticism, a desire for a check from the publishers, and a desire for more checks from future publishers.

So one can argue that even the blandest non-fiction text will have aspects of it that cause it to act as a tool to advance the author's agenda, even if only his professional fulfillment and personal satisfaction. Thus it must have some element of the performative, which asserts a purpose. But it is only able to accomplish any of this if it is able to induce its readers to enter rapport with it. In the same way a wrench is a tool for attaching and removing nuts and bolts. And a popular novel is a tool for invoking enjoyable emotions. And a political advertising campaign is a tool for exalting one faction of the power elite over another. The text is a lever to facilitate the installation of a desired circumstance. It is not the installation. It is not the circumstance. It is only a tool.

IV. Texts as Tools, and Vice-Versa

Texts are tools that enable the mind to crystallize meaning and spread it to other minds. "True" and "false" are a residue of the accomplishment of this performance—its "reviews," as it were. If the audience the text was aimed at generally accepts its meaning, it is "true"; otherwise it is "false."

The types of text may be conveniently classified into two categories—the advantageous and the exploitive—these determined by who prospers in the case of the text's general acceptance. With advantageous texts, both the author and the reader will prosper, the reader paying the author for the right to enjoy the benefits the text supplies: useful information or historical perspective, entertainment or instruction in some technique the reader may use to accomplish his or her will. On the other hand, there are texts that exploit by presenting information in such a way that the reader who enters rapport with them will be induced to act to promote the author's surreptitious purpose. By definition advertising lands in this category, as does all partisan political writing, including much that professes to be "academic" or "serious journalism." And much fiction should be included here, and not just *Uncle Tom's Cabin* or a Tom Clancy novel. Serious literature doesn't have to be non-partisan, just timeless, and artistry in language, imagery and metaphor can accomplish that. Shakespeare's *Henry V* projects a fabulous glamour, but with such words, who can care? It's best to love it for the art and just forget there ever was such a person as the butcher who besieged Rouen. It is safe for us to do so since the 15th century is long-gone, but to have loved the play at its premier would have been to succumb to Tudor propaganda, and devotion to their *status quo*.

To the extent that texts are effective at imposing meaning, they are effective as tools. Like a screwdriver. The question then becomes: when you buy a text, is it like buying a screwdriver to actualize your will to mechanical attachment, or is it instead as if you were making yourself available to someone else's will, and you're the one getting attached. *Who manipulates*—that is the thing to know about a text.

But if texts are tools, to what extent are tools like texts? Well, most obviously tools manipulate matter just as texts manipulate mind. More subtly, like texts tools are specific to a context—to their technologies and the nature of the raw materials these technologies exploit. There is nothing so worthless as an obsolete tool, one whose context no longer exists. Or an obsolete text, for that matter. Of course tools like wrenches and screwdrivers haven't changed much, or shovels, either, and there certainly are some texts that offer such a penetrating insight into the human condition that they will endure for centuries. But most don't, and soon are worthy for little more than wrapping fish or lining the bottom of birdcages. Just as sockets for bolting bridge girders together make great doorstops and bookends.

The point is that both texts and tools are abstractions that serve human intention, frozen, specific to perform their special purposes. The contexts for texts and tools, on the other hand—be they taste in fiction, engine design, political issues, products to be advertised, building materials, theological fashion, electronics technology, or paradigms of magick—never hold still. And when they change, the tools/texts meant to manipulate them turn obsolete, becoming a sort of residue, a fossil record that is harmless or even fascinating when viewed as a sequence of artifacts, but which becomes extremely dangerous when seen as any sort of repository of Truth.

But that's the big picture, and never more obvious than in our turbulent present. For most of human history the contingent nature of "Truth" was hidden behind a technical stability that damped out all but the strongest impulses toward both spiritual and physical innovation. Most everyone worked the land; one could go no faster than a good horse; wisdom was to be found in Homer, the Bible, or perhaps Aristotle or Aquinas. The greatest available power sources were the miller's wheel, the smith's forge, and the neighbor's oxen. Thus it had been, so it was, and so it seemed it would always be, forever until the end of time. But the past two hundred years have shown this *status quo* to be contingent indeed, vulnerable to any shift in technology, and thus apparently in the throes of dissolution in these last years of the 20th century. In any event, the times have demonstrated the inability of our honored texts to address our current circumstances. They are no more capable of providing a handle on existence than a steam piston can power a computer.

This brings us to the ontology part of this essay, the question of whether an actual Being—one to whose contours all knowledgeable men and women would conform—exists at all.

We have determined that there is no pure constative, that the production of any text is a performance done to advance a specific purpose that may have little or nothing to do with the "meaning" the text presents. But can we now jump from the inability to objectively describe existence to the unreality of existence? Does anything count beyond the intentions of the entities that perceive the universe and manipulate it to preserve and enhance their personal circumstances, according to their wills?

To answer this we need to know the origins of this notion of "existence." Only after we look from whence it has come can we know if we should expect it to stick around, or if we need to look for something more dynamic to suit our dynamic times.

V. Origins of Being

Now if Being is to be any sort of viable concept, we perforce must also have Truth—which is to say, a potential for acquiring an accurate notion of What Is. But "truth" is not a solid concept. In its etymology it is related to the words "truce," "trust" and "trow." This implies that it originally referred to human reliability, acts of veracity, and a willingness to rely on the assertions of others—keeping one's word, not betraying comrades, staying bought. The notion of "truth" as a proper way of understanding reality—a statement of *what is*—is a fairly recent application of the word. But then Anglo-Saxons have been fairly recent arrivals to the realms of civilization, and it has been in civic organizations that the notion of truth has had its important applications. Whether it has relevance to any other context remains to be seen.

But if *what is* is not what we instinctually affirm and respond to, what is it that induces us to act? To address this, it might be useful to return to the notion of rapport. In the first section I defined it as the mental state that allows us to accept as real the information coded in a test. At this point I'd like to expand it to include the acceptance of information from any alien source. What we enter rapport with determines our realities, and so defines our consciousness in any particular instance.

The type of human consciousness that came before the civic period was the tribal, and we can call it the first type, since it has apparently been operative since before the emergence of *Homo sapiens*. In tribal consciousness rapport is given to the elements of the natural world that the tribe must manipulate if it is to survive. One entered into rapport with the forest or the river and the creatures that lived there, tried to feel their awareness from their own perspective, and drew upon their knowledge and their power. This rapport was attained by treating these elements as living individuals rather than as dead phenomena that could be exploited without consequence, and the result was an intimate cooperation between humans and the natural world. And while the rapport was most effectively carried out on a psychic level, it was reinforced by ritual practice. If the bear was killed for food, its immortal soul was acknowledged and sent on its way with respect. If crops were planted and harvested, human sacrifice affirmed that our flesh, too, was grass. The objective world was not seen to "exist" but to "live," and that just as much as the deer or the bear or one's own children. The way to deal with this personalized world was through magick, and magick was as much a part of life as eating, sleeping and sex.

Civilized living made its appearance with the beginnings of large-scale agriculture, the exploitation of the earth to obtain maximum production. Along with civilization came written language, whether phonetic, ideographic or pictographic; Sumerians, Egyptians, Mayans, Cretans and Phoenicians all had scripts as soon as they had any architecture worthy of the name. And so they had texts, and with these they began to define existence—the way things had to *be*.

But with texts comes the question of truth. The forest and the river never lied. With them there was only the need to sustain the rapport, and the shaman who could do so had no need to fear that false knowledge or false power would come through. But rapport with a text brought no assurance of any real contact with the essence of the matter. Any text could be perverted. There could be fraudulent accounts, counterfeit warrants, corrupt laws, heretical revelations. These had to be exposed by comparison to what was really there: the real inventory, the real authority, the real political necessities, the real macrocosm. And so the notion of True Being came into usefulness, and people set out to discover it.

Of course on a mundane level, this concern over True Being was rooted in the question of *what* belongs to *whom*—not so very important to a hunter-gatherer, but of great moment once property began to be accumulated. What this concern called forth on a mundane level was all the apparatus of control intrinsic to civic culture. But on the more spiritual levels, the early civic response was much like the tribal. Since the source of the people's power was the civic organization, the city itself was personified through its god, and rapport was established through devotion to that deity. But for the city to be empowered by a *true god*, it had to be in sympathy with the *true universe*, the macrocosm—which is to say, the clockwork of the seven planets, the turning of the four seasons, the geometry of the six directions. And so the priests did their best to make the city imitate this macrocosm. The city would be laid out according to the cardinal points, the wall built on the sacred furrow, with the temple and the palace of the king and queen in the center. The king would serve as the embodiment of the city's patron deity, the queen as the goddess. This identification would be reenergized by periodic ritual sacrifice, either of the king, of a sacred stand-in (human or animal), or of the queen and her court in the rite of *suttee*. In effect, what this priestly construct provided was a model of the macrocosm that was much closer to home than the stars and planets. As Joseph Campbell described it, it was a middle cosmos—a mesocosm—between the macrocosm of the universe and the microcosms that are the citizens of a community. Through its institutionalized regularity, modeled on the universal regularity, regular living could be imposed on the unruly humans in a society, human nature aligned with Great Nature, and all human activity made definable in its terms. This sort of thinking survives even to modern times through the use of astrology, where one assumes that one does better if one aligns one's activity so it harmonizes with the motions of the planets against the stars, with the astrological experts serving in the priestly role, translating the austere clockwork of the planets and signs into terms relevant to human life.

    One thing this early civic model did not need was much in the way of text. The form was preserved in architecture, ritual procedure and the natural environment of the city's locale, and any text was more likely to be either a piece of magickal equipment (e.g., the Egyptian *Book of the Dead*), a chronicle, or a book of temple accounts than any sort of deep penetration into mystic truth. But such simplicity could not last. One thing this primal model requires is settled circumstances, for otherwise the physical aspects of the ritual alignment with the Greater Universe cannot be maintained. But this meant that any people pushed into exile, if they were to resist absorption by their oppressors, would have to come up with a non-spatial template to assure their special rapport with Great Nature. The wandering Jews, for instance, were forced by circumstances to textualize their connection to power, in that the fleshpots of Egypt had lured them away from their source of power at Mt. Moriah and then trapped them in bondage in Goshen. This text is the Torah, including the Law of Moses, a nice piece of work for that Egyptian-trained magician. On the Authority of the Voice of God, it defined the circle and the ritual of Israel and made the whole life of the community into a continuous invocation of Yahweh, the God before Whom one should have no others.

Later came the Talmud. This was an elaboration of the Law, its rigid walls of text defining Jewish life after it became clear that there could be no more focus at Jerusalem. And the spiritual interpretation was the Qabalah, especially as given in the *Zohar*. It saw the Torah as a coded blueprint for Creation and the Law as a magickal practice designed to mend the rupture in the Godhead caused by Adam's Fall, making the Jews the chosen instruments of repair. The community relied on rapport with its texts to maintain its coherence, the texts defining the individual's relation to the community and to God, and determining what he or she must do to keep that relationship intact. The mesocosm had become a book.

Christianity took this methodology and extended it to include all who participated in its sacraments, thus transcending the narrow bounds of ethnicity that confined the Jewish conception of existence. But at the same time the notion of exclusive Truth was extended, for by extending monotheism, they perforce spread texts that claimed for themselves the sanction of the One True God. There was One Truth, and it was dogma, and if you didn't conform your life to it you burned in hell. Thus the West attained the apotheosis of textual rapport, its permeation through all aspects of society. It is certainly no place to look for a dispassionate view of the question of existence outside the performative, or the validity of constative "truth."

A better place would be among the Classical Greeks, the first people to even try to think logically about what we and the universe might actually be.

VI. Being and Philosophy

The question of what this world we live in might actually consist of was foremost in early Greek thought. Thales of Miletus, the first philosopher, supposed that everything was made of water. This might seem somewhat simplistic, but water does readily exhibit all three states of normal matter—simultaneously, if the weather's right. Also, Thales' theory is the first recorded logical generalization (as opposed to a mythic one). Thales successor in the Milesian school, Anaximander, countered by saying that the source of all was the Indefinite; stresses within this Indefinite created hot and cold, dry and moist, and from these came matter. And Heraclitus of Ephesus suggested fire as the primal thing, right on the mark when we consider $E = mc^2$.

But of course fire isn't really a thing, but a process—a standing wave, as the physicists would say. This is perfectly consistent with Heraclitus, who saw fire not so much as any sort of original substance, but more as the dynamic archetype of All Things, "kindling in measures and going out in measures." (fragment 30) And of course we can't step in the same river twice. The river also is a process. We might even say it is a standing wave formed from a harmonious tension between opposites: evaporation and condensation, agitation and sedimentation, the force of gravity and water's natural tendency to form into spheres. And for Heraclitus, balance or tension or even strife between opposites was what sustained the world. Even so, most people are incapable of recognizing the essential place of struggle, how the same forces that pull things apart bring them back together in a renewed form—the essence of creative destruction.

And so with this the gauntlet was thrown down, for what Heraclitus describes is hardly Being at all, but instead a moving thing that grows and dies and is inherently full of conflict. And so philosophers called it Becoming. And it was clear that many didn't like it at all.

An explicit objection to Becoming was made by Plato in his *Philebus*, but it is a weak one, a quip more than an argument. He made it through a conversation between Socrates and Protarchus, this concerning "two natures—one self-existent, the other ever in want of something," the first "majestic ever," the other "inferior." Giving as a first example grown men and their youthful lovers, Socrates offers another pair, Being and Becoming, or (in Jowett's translation) "essence and generation." "And would you say," Socrates asks, "that generation is for the sake of essence, or essence for the sake of generation?" When Protarchus expresses confusion, Socrates clarifies his meaning by asking whether "shipbuilding is for the sake of ships, or ships for the sake of ship-building?" And then Socrates sums up, saying that "each generation is relative to, or for the sake of, some being or essence." (54)

Which is rather a specious argument, since the partisan of Becoming could reply that ships don't exist for shipbuilding but instead for *shipping*, for moving goods, people, animals, fish and so on over water, or else for the military interdiction of shipping, and using the water to move troops, horses, military stores and enginery of war. And all these are Becomings—generating creative change. Or, perhaps better, *Doings*. But since Plato was hardly a stupid person, we should look beneath his superficial argument to find his real agenda.

In my opinion Plato's real problem with Becoming is that it does not support a social order. The mesocosm, the middle cosmos, must have its foundation in a stable macrocosm—an Absolute Being—if the individual microcosms are to avoid degenerating into anarchy. And of course the assertion of this True Being—so exalted that only specially trained philosopher-kings could apprehend its essence—was a major innovation of Plato's philosophy. For him to admit that all was in flux—Becoming—would be to imply that the ruling class had no philosophical mandate to run things, but was merely part of a social dialectic (as it were), maintaining balance through its opposition to the proletariat. Plato's opposition to this philosophical formlessness is consistent with his life and writing. His mother and father both came from high-born Athenian families, and he was encouraged to take his part in conservative politics. He rejected this course due to the violence and mendacity inherent in a political career, but there's no indication he changed this political bias, even if he chose philosophy to advance it instead of statecraft.

Plato made a more reasoned reply to Heraclitus in his *Cratylus*, where he offers his response to Heraclitus alleged statement that all is in flux.

He begins (439) by having Socrates demand that Cratylus tell him "whether there is or is not any absolute beauty or good, or any other absolute existence." Cratylus replies that there is. But, Socrates goes on, absolute beauty or good cannot always be passing away like some superficial quality, nor can absolute beauty change at all, for "how can that be a real thing that is never in the same state?" (439) Besides that, things in flux cannot be known, and if all is in flux, one must wonder how there can be any knowledge at all. "But if that which knows and that which is known exist ever, and the beautiful and the good also exist, then I do not think they can resemble a process or flux, as we were just now supposing." (440)

And for Plato the existence of this *absolute good* was very important indeed, for he has Socrates declare in the *Republic* "that the idea of the good is the highest knowledge, and all other things become useful and advantageous only by their use of this." (6:505) Without an unchanging form or an absolute idea to embody this "good," there could be no knowledge of it, guidance by it, or beneficial effect from it. Flux becomes turmoil; process turns to anarchy.

Curiously, however, that last quotation has a variant form that is quite pertinent to our subject here. This variation is not found in Plato, but in an account of Socrates written by Socrates' student Xenophon. Xenophon was a soldier, historian and gentleman farmer as well as a friend of Socrates, and like Plato he was much more an aristocrat than a partisan of democracy. But he did not have Plato's high intellect, and so we might suppose him less likely to use philosophy to advance his political agenda. In any event, he had a sincere love for Socrates, and in his *Memoirs of Socrates* he recalls Socrates being asked just what the greatest thing was. And his Socrates gave an answer similar to the answer Plato quotes, but not quite the same.

As Xenophon described it, "Socrates being asked, 'What study was the most eligible and best for man?' answered, 'To *do well*.'" His questioner then asked "'If good fortune was the effect of study?'" Socrates rejected this possibility, defining good fortune as rewards that come without effort,

> "while the success that is the effect of study must always be preceded by long searching and much labor, and is what I call *doing well*: and I think," added Socrates, "that he who diligently applies himself to this study cannot fail of success; ...whereas they who will take no pains, neither can know anything perfectly, or do anything well; they please not the gods, and are of no use to man." (pp. 166–167)

In the chapter that follows this speech (III, 10), Xenophon describes how Socrates questioned three Athenian artisans to root out the crux of *doing well* in painting, sculpture, and the manufacture of body armor for combat. Socrates' conversation with Pistias the armorer nicely illustrates just what Socrates meant by that term.

Socrates begins by praising the contrivance of the armor's design, but then asks Pistias why his armor costs more when the materials are the same as those used by other armorers. Pistias replies that his is better proportioned, to which Socrates asks how this proportion might be found. "Not by weight or measure: for as you make for different people, the weight and the size must likewise differ, or they will not fit." Besides, not all bodies are justly proportioned, so Socrates asks, "How can you make a well-proportioned suit of arms for an ill-proportioned body?"

"I make it fit," Pistias replies, "and what fits is well-proportioned."

"Then you are of the opinion," Socrates agrees, "that when we declare anything well-proportioned, it must be in reference to the use for which it was intended." But then he has doubts and asks, "since the position of the body is not always the same, being

sometimes stooping and sometimes erect, how can the arms, that are made with such exactness, be at all times easy?"
"Neither can they," Pistias replies.
"You think then, Pistias, the arms which are well made are not those which are exact, or sit close to the body, but give the least trouble to him who wears them?"
"You think so," Pistias concludes, "and have certainly taken the matter right." (pp. 171–172)

I should also note here that the difference between Plato's "the idea of the good" and Xenophon's "doing well" is not just a matter of two different translators' choices of words. Plato refers to *"Tou agathou idea," agathou* being the genitive form of the noun for "good." Xenophon, on the other hand, uses the word *"eupraxia,"* "well-practice." *"Eu"* is a prefix found in such English words as "euphony" and "eupepsia," for pleasant sound and healthy digestion. Thus it may not be made to stand alone like *agathou*, but must be applied to some specific action. Plato's Socrates is an idealist, while Xenophon's is a pragmatist.

Xenophon's *Memoirs* are full of encounters like the one between Socrates and Pistias, the philosopher meeting people, questioning their intent, and then showing how their intent either does or does not square with their circumstances, or how it does or does not square with what they are actually doing. While Plato and Xenophon agree with each other concerning the facts of Socrates' life (most notably his trial and execution and his reaction to his fate), Xenophon does not recount any of the abstruse philosophizing that is the staple in Plato, and makes no reference to the forms or any other philosophical absolutes. It is possible, of course, that Xenophon just wasn't invited to these conversations, just as Plato could have disdained to tag along when Socrates visited the merchants and politicians, sculptors and armorers. But it is also possible that Socrates wasn't as interested in Cosmic Truth as Plato said he was, and that he used the dialectic mostly for questioning his fellow Athenians, acting as the city's gadfly, which is of course just how he referred to himself. One simply has to wonder whom to believe. But if I'm going to question Plato's veracity, I should surely note this passage from his *Phaedrus*, where he has Socrates chiding Phaedrus:

> There was a tradition in the temple of Dodona that oaks first gave prophetic utterances. The men of old, unlike in their simplicity to young philosophy, deemed that if they heard the truth even from 'oak or rock' it was enough for them; whereas you seem to consider not whether a thing is or is not true, but who the speaker is and from what country the tale comes. (275)

In our present context this speech is loaded with more irony than just the Socratic. Besides the irony "Socrates" directs at "Phaedrus," we have that which accompanies the question of Plato's own accuracy as a reporter of what Socrates actually said. And then there's even more if we consider that truth must always be more doubtful when its source is a speaker of words than when that source is an emanator of elemental energy. Oaks and rocks let you know what you need to *do well* within their domains, and then give you the power to do it, if you have the power to take it. Speakers of truth, on the other hand, offer a semblance of their particular angle on *what is*, bent into words according to their purposes—malignant or benign, self-inflated or self-reflective, and always tainted with some bias. *These* words certainly are.

Platonism met Jewish monotheism with the Ptolemys, and made a formal coupling with Christianity through the appropriation of the concept of the *logos* by the author of the Gospel of John, this reinforced by the writings of the early Church Fathers. Thus the notion of Absolute Being was driven into the Western psyche so deeply that even the most anti-Christian thinkers never questioned it. It is only within the chaos of our own century that any have come to doubt it.

The chaos has forced the issue, for it has called into question the notion of anything absolute, and all pretense of stability. The traditional mesocosm was held together by economic necessity and political and religious conservatism, but the two latter depend on the former and one year's economic necessity can be turned into the next year's obsolescence by a slight shift in technology.

Although technology was essentially static for millennia, since the industrial revolution it's been churning like a white-water river. The river that is never the same is moving faster and faster, and our mesocosmic raft was not made for waterfalls. We may yet need to sprout wings and fly.

VII. Doing

So what have we got?

First of all, and what should by now be obvious, is that there can be no objectivity in text. This was not unexpected, but as we have uncovered it, it's become clear there's no evidence for objectivity anywhere else, either. It didn't show up on the historical record until Plato and his colleagues abstracted it out of what they found important to think about. In tribal times, people saw the outside world as an aggregation of powers—elementals—all of which had personal lives analogous to their own. Thus for them reality was fundamentally *subjective*. The forest had interests and a perspective as much as the hunter, and though it had a more diffuse influence over the entities within its sphere, it wasn't any less a person. Instead, the notion of objective reality doesn't show up until our ancestors invented civil society, when the need for an objective determination of questions of property became critical. With that it became necessary to assert the existence of a stable macrocosm that included all True Being, this for the political purpose of establishing human society as a model of it, a mesocosm. This assumption of objective Being was sustained and seemingly confirmed by the apparent stability of the "outside" world, a stability that had its foundation in the regular motion of the heavenly bodies, in the apparent immutability of species (as if they had been created all at once, or perhaps in six days' time), and also in the static condition of human technology, economy and political culture. There did seem to be a True Existence, and it could be found by any who were sufficiently diligent and holy to discover it.

But that's all over now. Technology has shot itself into the outer planets. The world is a borderless ocean of goods, cash and "securities," churned by currents economists barely comprehend. Political culture is a mere remnant of the old mesocosmic stability. Even the origins of species are coming under human domination, and what the "objective" world might become is anybody's guess.

And beyond these historical considerations, and all other logical argument, there is a counter to objectivity far more primal: the fact that no one has ever been "outside." All knowledge, all discursive assertion of anything, is through consciousness, and even after we grant that there are other consciousnesses as fundamental as ours looking out from every other pair of eyes we meet, that only means that whatever goes on behind them suffers from the same limitations that we ourselves must endure. Which is to say, there is no apparent experience more fundamental than our own. And if the mountains have awareness, it will be appropriate to the needs of their mountainous situations—that is, no more objective than anyone else's.

The materialist may counter here that all my arguments are mere speculation, and well he should, but then so is his dry assertion of Being, and there is no more proof for one than for the other. The proof lies in the power you can get out of it, and that contest is far from over.

But if it isn't all Being, then what is it?

I will not say Becoming, since that implies an action too random or undirected to be consistent with our obviously well-designed circumstances. Instead I will offer *Doing*, presenting us with a universe of process, with all aspects of manifestation pursuing some goal, more or less distant, more or less intelligently. Doing gives us a universe that is dynamic on all levels, driven by an implied purpose, and hence an implicit intelligence, and this is surely consistent with the self-driven contrivance of physical nature. It is also the most useful for our turbulent time, what with our desperate need to replace the crumbling mesocosm with some cohering principle that is nonetheless capable of encouraging individual creativity. After all, Doing is consistent with the teaching of the pragmatic Socrates described by Xenophon, and so provides us with a standard for excellence that does not depend on any metaphysical Absolutes. Instead of learning "the idea of the good," we must simply begin to "do well," a notion familiar to wizards of all stripes.

Historically, Doing was first explicitly offered as "that which exists independently" by the English sorcerer Peter J. Carroll, this in his *Psychonomicon*, where he states, "There is no being, all is doing." (p. 88) But in this he was implicitly preceded by Aleister Crowley, or rather Aiwass, for in *Liber AL vel Legis* we read:

> Do what thou wilt shall be the whole of the Law.
> Thou hast no right but to do thy will.
> Do that and no other shall say nay.

And Crowley himself suggested that reality is not Being but *Going*. In Going we have a process similar to Doing, with the implied "goer" serving like the implied "doer" as a locus self-awareness. "Come unto me is a foolish word, for it is I that go."

The magickal implications of this shift from Being to Doing are profound. There is no Absolute Reality to which we must make an effort to conform; what we have all around us is what has transpired as the result of past doings, open to alteration by whatever we may try next. The "results to date" (as we may call the present reality) are the product of a collective effort; we have shared the work with the birds and trees and life of the stars, as well as with our fellow humans. We are Eyes of God, and at the deepest center of our awareness, we touch it all.

Now this might seem a meaningless pantheism, except that properly applied it will make the machinery of manifestation available for manipulation by any who are capable of recognizing that machinery, and who have the courage to come into rapport with it. Before the Beginning we Ourselves set up the mechanisms. We contrived them so they would operate to facilitate the creation of a universe that would conform to Our Requirements. Now we need only re-member them. If we can hark back to the appropriate atavisms at the necessary depths of consciousness, we will find all the power we need in order to accomplish whatever the Doing of our wills requires. This is an act of recollection. We left it that way at the beginning and it will be ready when we turn back for it.

A strange way to look at it, but these are strange times, and demand bizarre expediencies.

Finally, let us look at the notion of enlightenment to see how it will be affected by our shift from Being to Doing.

In the tradition of Being, enlightenment is the union of the mystic's individual consciousness with the Consciousness of the Absolute, also called God. It is an identification of Self with All Things, this accomplished by an annihilation of all that is limited about that Self. This presupposes a cessation of desire and an attainment of an inner peace that allows the mystic to appreciate the Truth that transcends crass and clamorous appearance. It is an elevation above the turbulent round of birth-reproduction-death and also a dispassionate appreciation of that round. It is as placid as Eternity and as static, as static as human technology for the 5000 years that preceded the middle ages.

To be static now is to be left in a ditch.

To put this Enlightenment of Being into the terms we've been using, we might say it is an immediate rapport of the microcosm with the macrocosm, without the need for a mesocosm to align or adjust the interaction. In practice, such a rapport was often more easily established in the mesocosm's absence, and hence the profusion of ascetics in the forest, hermits on the mountain, and stylites perched on pillars in the desert. Stillness of mind was needed to comprehend the fullness of All Things; involvement in personal affairs disturbs the mind; and so the cessation of all action was required. Non-action was thus a yogic virtue, just as the good Christian shunned the World, the Flesh and the Devil. In this case there is not all that much difference between East and West.

Now I should stress here that the mystic's retreat from the mesocosm was not required because the mesocosm itself was somehow flawed or illusory or corrupt. The problem was that it had always been a bit inadequate for the job. It was only capable of whipping teeming humanity into a bare semblance of holiness, so the mystic who craved the real thing did better to step outside to where the connection to the macrocosm was up to himself alone, and so comparatively easy to realize.

But now the old mesocosm has gone from inadequacy to total collapse, and there's no place left to be alone anymore. All the stability once imposed by tradition has been made obsolete by the explosion of technical innovation and the consequent abrogation of all implicit social contracts. The marketplace has metastasized, overwhelming the temple and wall that defined the center and perimeter of the old mesocosm. In fact, temple and wall are even now being dismantled to facilitate and even feed this expansion, and so it works to penetrate into every crevice of human experience. Even the wilderness has been co-opted. It has become either a place to be exploited commercially or else a pristine jewel, a one-of-a-kind ecological treasure that might be imperiled by the cooking fires of wandering hermits. There is no refuge left, and the marketers' chorus is heard on every crag and moor, chanting their paean so all may hear and want and buy.

But that's just a problem for mystics, who lose their focus when the world intrudes. For sorcerers, on the other hand, there remains the churning energy of it all. And when it thrusts itself upon us, that is energy we can capture and convert to power to accomplish our wills.

So I would propose a new notion of enlightenment better suited to our new notion of reality, to wit: enlightenment is not a state of identity with Absolute Being, but the attainment of a momentum that is in synch with the overall current of Doing. If you can recognize the power in your doings and then accelerate that power so it enters into rapport with the flow of power all around you, you will become able to perceive power's every nuance, and so gain the discrimination to take whatever you need of it, whenever you need it.

So the key to enlightenment shifts from non-action to action. But it must be a special sort of action, attuned to the dynamics of the energy of attention, which is magickal power. We must work to keep our action from being corrupted by any sort of limited emotional or ideological motivation. It must be the result of an inner imperative to act, not the consequence of a logical, reasoned strategy. Discursive thought can never be more than a tool, an act of after-the-fact bookkeeping, or a façade on the flow of power. In the context of power, what matters is the intent that focuses the energy, the consistency of the energy's purpose, its fluidity and clarity, its strength and endurance, whether it is prone to act or waits to react, and whether or not it is sympathetic to your will. But though these may all be described, that's just keeping records. Competent management only comes with direct perception and response, from a rapport with power in all the ways it moves around you. If you can't act until you've explained it to yourself, you're surely too slow.

Of course since discursive thought does not apply, one might be tempted to presume that this realm is beyond text, thus rendering essays like this one inappropriate. And yet the bookkeeping function can be helpful if it tells us what to look for in real time, and thus written accounts of sorcerous dynamics can be helpful to those interested in mastering them. If an author can abstract out the dynamic elements of empowered experience, he or she will be able to offer the reader techniques for manipulating power that the reader may apply if he or she has sorcerous ambitions. The reader can simply try them and see what happens, using trail and error to fine-tune the effects so they suit his or her specific psychic circumstances.

The texts that contain techniques like these may be found among the literature of the hard-core occult. The techniques have been recorded in text without significant distortion of effect because the methods themselves make no attempt to impose any specific notion of reality—Being or Doing or whatever—on those who would apply them. Rather, they deal with processes and relationships between processes, describing ways of manipulating power within the sorcerer's psyche and also between the sorcerer's psyche and the other awarenesses—spiritual, biological and elemental—that surround it upon this mundane sphere. Such relationships and the effects that are spawned out of them are all wrapped up in intention. Hence they are steeped in the performative, and the textual mode is utterly appropriate. The author of a technique ideally will have the intent of getting you to buy it and then try it, just to see what happens. And then, seeing what might be done, do more of it until you can find all the technique you need on your own and have no more need of texts, except of course for your magickal record.

Now admittedly this is the ideal for occult literature, and there is much that falls short. In many texts the techniques for handling power are concealed beneath the author's obsolete notions of Being; sometimes authors even draw moral or technical conclusions from such notions. But the person who is doing his or her will should be able to brush these façades aside to discover the operational dynamics that make a technique an effective one. Which is not to say you should be looking here. This text is much too theoretical to provide any of that sort of thing, and should be considered only an introduction to that more technical literature. We can just call it a signboard, pointing out an interesting byway through the psychic landscape.

With perhaps a little neon.

My thanks go to Hal von Hofe for his help with the Greek.

For Those Who Would Subvert The Status Quo

I. The End of the Game

For those who recognize themselves in the title, there need be no justification for what follows. The commercial, political and cultural establishment as it exists today is venal, decadent, corrupt, and wholly resistant to reform. The rich get richer; the poor get poorer; you get the best justice money can buy; and the prime avenues for success in business life are organized specifically to nullify the Self. The apparent struggles in political life (ecologists vs. developers, pro-life vs. pro-choice, welfare vs. self-reliance) are essentially side-shows, since the controversies are solely about the details of the system and have nothing to do with its essential structure. The system is open, to be sure. It admits anyone willing to trade their integrity for the privilege of participating in it. Outside agitators are tolerated for their novelty value, but are seen as no real threat since as soon as they get powerful enough to be significant, established powers will co-opt their message, then commercialize it or otherwise make it trivial enough to be painlessly absorbed by the status quo. Then those who originated the outside movement are given the choice (sometimes) of either a personal co-option or else criminality, self-destruction, and/or voluntary oblivion.

Those who reject my assessment may reply that it's been going on for five thousand years, and that what I would subvert is the

Game of Civilization itself. I would reply that this is not the case. The Game of Civilization is over. It's over, but the winners don't want to start a new one, preferring to sit on their winnings even as "What Comes Next" presses us all up against the future. But if we don't start the next Game soon, it will be too late, and something will break.

The Game of Civilization is over because it is no longer necessary, having been rendered technologically obsolete. For the Powers That Be to persist in a parody of that Game in order to maintain their privileged status is to waste time, lives and resources. In the long run this will imperil our species and even life on the planet.

That the Game of Civilization is over becomes clear once we consider why people began to play it. It certainly wasn't anything the human race rushed into. The dating of sophisticated cave art has pushed the presence of self-reflective humanity back before 20,000 b.c.e., and the cultivation of grain has been dated to 8000 b.c.e., but large-scale agriculture did not begin until the cities of Mesopotamia appeared around 3200 b.c.e. Assuming these people weren't stupid, why did they wait over 4000 years to go from knowing how to plant grain to making the commitment to live off it, especially since agriculture is so much more efficient than hunting and gathering food from the wild?

I would suggest it's because hunting and gathering food is a combination of picnic and adventure, and agriculture is boring, backbreaking stoop work. Of course the working of small garden plots goes back to the Paleolithic, but growing vegetables to supplement food taken from the wild is a lot less effort than growing enough grain to supply most of one's diet, and food for the stock animals as well. So it is reasonable to assume that people only took up large-scale agriculture because they were forced to. Geological evidence suggests that it was drought that made them do it. The great deserts of Africa and Asia were once well-watered prairies, but with the retreat of the glaciers they gradually began to dry up, forcing the people who hunted game there to congregate in the valleys of the Nile, Euphrates and Indus. The only way they could feed themselves in this limited area was through organized agriculture. And so was man expelled from the Garden, obliged to eat bread in the sweat of his face until he returns to the dust from whence he came.

It remained this way for five thousand years, until we made our machines and mastered them, and no longer needed to dig dirt to live.

But we go ahead of ourselves here, for the technique of planting seed and irrigating crops was just the beginning. For it to be efficient, it had to be organized on a large scale, which meant there had to be lots of people digging dirt and a few telling them where and how to dig it. Also, the efficient production of food allowed for people to specialize in other technologies—pottery, metalwork, the weaving of cloth, the cutting of stone. Thus was "wealth" invented, treasure that had to be defended against both domestic thieves and foreign marauders—those who found war to be a more pleasant occupation than digging dirt. And since drilled soldiers defend better than an armed mob, even more organization was required, a hierarchal chain of command that could compel men to stand and fight instead of do the more natural thing and run away.

Thus was civilization born, and politics also, since with armies came the gun that political power grows out of. Now everyone could be told how best to dig dirt, build granaries and fortifications, and attack and defend as required by strategy and law. Whether king or slave, priest or soldier, digger of dirt or caster of bronze, each individual had a role to play in the *civitas*, and to the extent they were devoted to their roles, the civic entity prospered and the individuals with it. To be devoted in this case basically meant that one knew one's place and stayed in it. There was no hypocrisy in this criterion. Since the community really did have places for everyone, most found their spots and made sacrifice to the civic god to ensure the prosperity of the civic entity. Those few who disdained the community were obliged to make their ways without it, either as rebels, romantics or hermits. The first two generally died young; the last became renowned for wisdom and spiritual power. They were, after all, the only ones with any real perspective on things.

Everyone else was *of* their culture, a part of its organic wholeness. The prosperity of the people depended upon their devotion to their civic entity; its survival depended upon its capacity for returning this devotion as efficient organization capable of fulfilling the needs of the citizenry and defending against foreign threat.

It was a productive arrangement, tending to promote social stability, but now sadly obsolete. With the technological revolution of the past three centuries, what was once essential is now superfluous. Once gangs of men were needed to reap grain, gangs of women were needed to weave cloth, gangs of scribes to calculate accounts, and regiments of soldiers to hold ground. Now crops are harvested with giant combines, cloth is woven on looms as big as a house, computers manage the accounts and the inventory as well, and war between sovereign states so tends to annihilate that it is grossly impractical as a way of accomplishing political or economic goals.

So there are now no roles to fill. There is Capital and it uses machines or humans as need dictates, according to what is most efficient as determined by Capital's sole criterion: the bottom line. Purchase price, depreciation, property tax and maintenance may be calculated against training costs, salary, employment taxes and health care—the inorganic widget compared to the organic with no loss of precision. And if the structure of society disintegrates as the dispossessed split off from it in an attempt to feed upon it, that's what prisons are for, the added tax burden just another expense to be factored into the cost of doing business. Of course with lethal injection so much more humane than shock, gas or rope, might there not be a technological fix here as well?

II. Mesocosms

"Mesocosm" means "middle cosmos." It is a word used by Joseph Campbell (in his *Masks of God* series) to denote the sociological middle ground between objective reality (the macrocosm) and the individual (the microcosm). In Campbell's sense the mesocosm is an attempt by a people to order their society so it mirrors their understanding of the order of the cosmos, especially as this order is displayed in the motion of the heavenly bodies. People did this in the hope that such schemes would bring the unruly individuals who made up their societies into synch with the eternal order of the universe.

The mesocosm is the invention of civilization. When people still lived as tribes in the wild there was no need for it. Order was provided by the bonds of kinship and the necessity of maintaining a psychic rapport with the elements of the natural world, a rapport established through the guidance of the tribe's shamans. But the technologies of civilization make rapport with the natural world unnecessary and even inefficient. A tribe in rapport with the forest might be able to live off it, but a civilization can cut it down, coke the wood to charcoal to smelt iron, then use that iron to make the weapons that kill all the tribespeople who refuse to become the slaves who dig the dirt to grow the crops to feed themselves and their civilized overlords as well.

Civilization's problem is not establishing rapport with nature, but maintaining the order within its own society that allows it to efficiently exploit nature. This order had to be something greater than human, for if it were only human each person would define his or her priorities in personal terms, organization would be a matter of personal convenience, and society would be ripe for destruction. The idea that one could find more profound guidance in the greater cosmos an ancient one, and is well-stated in Plato's *Timaeus*. From the translation of Benjamin Jowett:

> When a man is always occupied with the cravings of desire and ambition, and is eagerly striving to satisfy them, all his thoughts must be mortal... But he who has been earnest in the love of knowledge and of true wisdom...must have thoughts immortal and divine..., and since he is ever cherishing the divine power, and has the divinity within him in perfect order, he will be singularly happy. Now there is only one way of taking care of things, and this is to give each the food and motion which are natural to it. And the motions which are naturally akin to the divine principle within us are the thoughts and revolutions of the universe.

These each man should follow, and correct the courses of the head which were corrupted at our birth... (90)

By Campbell's account "the thoughts and revolutions of the universe" were most often brought down to earth through urban planning, ritual emulation of divine behavior, and a close study of the motion of the planets against the stars. Urban planning could be something like the laying out of the city according to the four cardinal points, with the royal palace and the god's temple in the center. Of course the temple and the palace were often the same, for the king and queen could be seen as the earthly incarnation of the god and goddess, with their ritual intercourse helping to make the land fruitful and the harvest secure. And at least in the earliest periods, the king might from time to time be sacrificed in emulation of the dying sun, his younger replacement representing the vigor of the sun reborn in spring. But whatever the rites, their timing would be determined by the motions of the heavens, the divine source of earthly power.

In Egypt this divinely instituted order was called ma'at. In China it was Tao, in India dharma. In ancient Israel it was the Law.

By embodying this divine order in the political and religious life of the community, by creating this mesocosm, the priest-kings of antiquity turned the whole life of their domains into an ongoing magickal rite, a ritual that encouraged each of their citizens to devote their lives to their particular roles in society—to enter rapport with them, in fact. Thus was the order of society secured. And so it remained for three thousand years.

The first telling blow against this arrangement was made by a Jew from Nazareth named Yeshua, who declared that we should give to Caesar what is Caesar's, and to God what is God's, thus initiating the separation of Church from State. This crack was plastered over with the triumph of Christianity, emperors and kings taking it upon themselves to rule by the Grace of God, but the precedent had been set and the damage done. This became obvious with the Protestant Reformation, when the catholicity of the Roman Church was broken by the ambitions of princes and the doctrinal innovations of individual believers, resulting in the plethora of Christian denominations we know today. Apart from the turmoil occasioned by the schisms themselves, this fragmentation had little effect on the unity of society. The State focused on war and the economic development that sustained it; the various churches united to teach obedience to temporal authority, even as they disagreed about their respective interpretations of scripture. But then came the industrial revolution, the revolution of modern thought (Adam Smith, Charles Darwin, Karl Marx, Sigmund Freud, Albert Einstein), and also the slaughter of modern industrial warfare. Suddenly there were no heavens to emulate anymore, only the sciences of interchangeable matter and energy and the oh so frail human psyche, all held in place by self-interest and the hard hand of the State.

It isn't enough. Now that the mesocosm has been broken, it is obvious why it was necessary in the first place. Without it, the Game of Civilization must end. But it is a Game that the Powers That Be must perpetuate if they are to maintain their privileged status, and so will they build their mesocosm from whatever material they can find, even if these constructions have more to do with desire and ambition than the immortal and divine.

III. The Totality

In the title of this essay I make mention of a "status quo" that those sympathetic to my message might wish to subvert. At one point in history this status quo and the powers who managed it were perfectly identifiable entities—the propertied classes, the princes of State and Church, the intellectuals who served them, etc.—but not anymore. Today, thanks largely to the triumph of bourgeois political values, this privileged status is open to anyone with the cash to buy in. The resulting edifice might seem monolithic, and from the perspective of those who are outside it, it often acts as if it were indeed a unity, but for those who are involved in it, it is nothing of the sort—more like rats feeding in a bucket of corn.

They struggle amongst themselves, by the rules they call Law, and call this freedom for all. They are fragmented, but generally all moving in the same direction. As for their relations with the State, there is an alliance without any real union. Each is *of* the other without being *in* it. The State is the ultimate enforcer of commercial behavior, and yet depends on commerce for its very existence. Commerce is constrained by the State and taxed, but the order the State imposes provides an environment where commerce may be conducted with minimal risk. Political competition is a façade upon less conspicuous tides of economic dominance. Political power may grow out of the barrel of a gun, but money buys guns.

Of course in essence this is the way it has always been; those who control the means of production have tremendous influence over the means of control. What makes our own time so particularly venal is the way commercial responsibility has been taken from individuals and institutionalized, which for all practical purposes is to nullify it. Responsibility is now held by financial fictions, legal golem, Frankenstein monsters called "limited liability corporations." "Limited liability" means only financial responsibility, and money (after all) is only an *abstraction* of value, a passing effect on the bottom line, spiritually null and devoid of all intrinsic consequence. Legal golem have no spirit to be encrusted with karma, no souls to be saved or damned, no guilt, no shame, not even any essential identities to carry enduring reputations, so easily may they merge and divest. They assume all responsibility for the human acts committed in their names, thus absorbing it. And then they abstract it to nothingness, in the process absolving all but the most dispensable employees. They make it possible to "just do one's job" for No One at all. A corporation's employees are loyal to No One, act according to the policy of No One, and as they do so they are thus implicated in the acts of No One. For there is No One there. There is only an enduring bit of market pressure tied into a self-perpetuating legal convention in such a way that it reifies as infrastructure, workforce and product.

The counter to this is that it is the corporate officers who are responsible for the acts of the institution, but in practice they are only well-compensated technicians. Where once a Medici or a Carnegie could look upon his works and feel either fear or comfort for his soul, now they're just doing their jobs, counting the beans for old Synergistic Megaglom, Inc. Loyalties can no longer be personal, but must ultimately be directed to the health of the corporate body, to "the stockholders"—or, more precisely, to the stock *price* as an abstraction of the will of these nebulous proprietors—and so their most immediate priorities cannot aim beyond the next quarter's earnings.

It's not as if these people have any choice in the matter, either, once having chosen this road. If their primary loyalties are not to the bottom line, the corporation will find persons more willing to serve it. It is survival of the fittest, and the fittest are the ones who can obtain the best return on capital. The notion that economic stability is essential to the very health of society is irrelevant to them if by exploitation or turbulence they can better address their markets—but always the Market in the most abstract sense, which is to say, the most inhumane.

Thus the social classes that once had an interest in encouraging the culture to look toward eternity are now themselves transfixed on the mundane—as if they were some Gnostic Sophia enamored of her reflection on the mud. And as they fix their gaze there, so do they write their laws there, and find their politicians there. The mesocosm as template from Eternity is gone.

But it would be too much to say that the mesocosm as such has been obliterated. There's too much order even now for that to be the case. No, it isn't so much that the mesocosm has been destroyed, more that it has been turned inside out. Rather than purify the aspirations of humankind, this new, twisted mesocosm degrades them. The Powers That Be need something that will distract people's sights instead of elevate them, allowing them to identify with an ideal focused entirely on the satisfaction of desire. And in keeping with the new technology, this modern mesocosm delivers its message directly into our homes 24 hours each day. All we have to do is switch it on.

And with this we confront **the Totality**, omnipresent purveyor of commercial truth. "The Totality" is the name for the Media Presence used by "Hakim Bey," a pseudonymous prose poet and political theorist who has an apparently close connection to the art scene in Manhattan. He is an anarchist with an occult flavor, but though he includes a paean to sorcery in an early (and fairly well-known) series of essays called *Chaos: The Broadsheets of Ontological Anarchism*, he never discusses sorcerous technique, only strategy and mood. Among his better known strategies are "poetic terrorism" (which is given a section in the *Broadsheets*) and the "Temporary Autonomous Zone," or TAZ. But these are for later. What concerns us now is his notion of the Totality: the Media as parasitic purveyor of glamour, feeding off the people who are the most creative so it can both emasculate them and use their power to maintain its hold over the consuming masses.

Bey gives the Totality a brief, functional definition in the essay "Involution," included among his *Radio Sermonettes*:

> It's become a truism to say that society no longer expresses a consensus (whether reactionary or liberatory), but that a false consensus is expressed *for* society; let's call this false consensus "the Totality." The Totality is produced through mediation and alienation, which attempt to subsume or absorb all creative energies *for* the Totality...
>
> The Totality isolates individuals and renders them powerless by offering only illusory modes of social expression, modes which seem to promise liberation and fulfillment but in fact end by producing more mediation and alienation. This complex can be viewed clearly at the level of "commodity fetishism," in which the most rebellious or avant-garde forms in art can be turned into fodder for PBS or MTV or ads for jeans and perfumes.

"The Totality is produced through mediation and alienation." The very act of mediation—of taking a living, creative presence and recording, editing and repackaging it for broadcast between the ads—strips that presence of its intrinsic power and renders it a simulacrum of its original essence. The form that's left after the power is gone is still fit to distract the viewers' attentions, at least for awhile, that form having been a growth out of its original power. But none of that power, what Bey called a work's "auric content," is passed on to the populace at large. All they receive is simulation: two-dimensional projections of pixilated color, stereo interweaving of digitized sound, a whole electronic conjuration meant to induce rapport with what are essentially dead texts. Well-produced conjurations, to be sure; without high production values rapport could not be attained. Emotionally exciting texts, of course; without emotional excitement the populace might shift its attention to real reality, and grow rebellious. The people must be led to think they have lives beyond commerce, but must be discouraged from actually attempting to live such lives, lest they question their roles as elementary consumers within the greater corporate organism. All their attention must be directed to the mediated simulation, even as their actual contact with the immediate world is reduced to routine—a condition wherein they are essentially blind to its power. What's on television is to be seen as entertaining and up-to-date; what's on the street is either unknown/dangerous or else ordinary. The theme park is exciting and fun; the forest and the desert and the weather on the mountain are something to drive through to get there. The structured world of office or school, service club or church-of-your-choice is socially valid; the elemental presence of the means of production is somewhere abroad.

Now for any mesocosm to function effectively, it must persuade the citizenry that they do best when they conform to its status quo. For 5000 years the condition to which one had to conform was the agricultural year of one's particular locale, and the local myths reflected this condition's numinosity. At present, however, what must be conformed to is the corporate regimentation of what Bey calls "Too-late Capitalism." And alienation from the numinous is what this conformity requires. Since the corporate status quo can have no auric content (there being No One there to generate it), the mesocosm that idealizes it can hardly inspire any either. But there is no risk of this happening with the Totality! The necessary alienation is accomplished automatically through the process of mediation, which splits off and discards the numinous quality of any artifact it represents. Thus the attention the Totality inspires is utterly venal, and not just through television. It has more devious tools than just that. Bey goes on:

> On a subtler level, however, the Totality can absorb and redirect any power whatsoever simply by re-contextualizing and re-presenting it. For instance the liberatory power of a painting can be neutralized or even absorbed simply by placing it in the context of a gallery or museum, where it will automatically become a mere *representation* of liberatory power. The insurrectionary gesture of a madman or criminal is not negated only by locking up the perpetrator, but even more by allowing the gesture to be represented—by a psychiatrist or by some brainless Kop-show on channel 5 or even by a coffee table book on art brut.

The Totality is a whore after anything new in art, technology, psychology and so on, but once the Totality seduces the new thing, that thing is drained. In the process of mediating it, of re-presenting it within the Totality's commercial context, the Totality appropriates its true essence to provide the Totality with a moment's true power to energize the shining façade it uses to hide the essential emptiness of its dead texts. Hence its appetite is insatiable, for the continuous reanimation of this façade is essential for its functioning as mesocosm. Here we see the Totality's fundamental weak point, for without this constant influx of energy it is in danger of exhaustion, followed by popular disinterest and mesocosmic collapse.

But then some media are more tightly tied to the Totality than others. Bey uses capital-intensity as a rough guide to the Totality's dominance over any particular textual vector—the more Capital a medium requires to accomplish its function, the more it will be a tool of the Totality. Thus the medium least under its influence is print, as shown by the existence of 'zines, comix, and self-published texts on sorcery. On the other hand, the medium most involved with the Totality is television, capital-intensive to an extreme, a tool perfectly designed to accomplish the Totality's purpose of a mass rapport with commerce. The video-tube acts as a magnet for attention to a far greater extent than music, print, or even the movie screen, which so dominates that its display must be visually interesting if it is to keep from being repellent. But the video-tube sucks attention into itself regardless of content. It is also the most all-pervasive of media, with a presence in nearly every home, school, tavern and motel room in America. Even so, television is only one of the Totality's available vectors. To generalize, we might say that the prime vehicle for the Totality is simply "journalism"—that which creates attractive texts and packages them for placement between the ads.

Bey offers the media coverage of the 1991 Gulf War as an example of the way the Totality performs its mesocosmic function. He notes that while millions of Americans were enlightened enough to oppose this conflict (begun by a nation that was America's erstwhile ally against the dread Iran, I might add), "the Media …produced (i.e., simulated) the impression that virtually no opposition to Bush's war existed or could exist." There was no peace "movement" because the media made it clear to each individual who opposed the war that he or she was alone, the only one who thought such stupid thoughts, "isolated, weird, queer, wrong, and finally non-existent." Bey sums up:

> This process of fragmentation has reached near-universal completion in our society, at least in the area of social discourse. Each person engages in a "relation of involution" with the spectacular simulation of Media. That is, our "relation" with Media is essentially empty and illusory, so that even when we seem to reach out and perceive reality in Media, we are in fact merely driven back in upon ourselves, alienated, isolated and impotent.

Through rapport with the Totality we engage in a shadow play with their manufactured world, and through it we think we know reality, even as the real world and all its power wait outside forgotten. Even when the Totality's display seems most disrespectful of the Powers That Be, even when it appears rebellious, even then it helps maintain them by encouraging us to believe that the necessary disrespect and rebellion have been taken care of, and all we need do is sit and watch some more.

And buy, of course.

IV. Origins of the Totality

One flaw in Bey's presentation and in my own also has been the way we've set up the Totality up as a sort of monolithic Moloch that was somehow born fully-grown out of Capital—which is to say, out of an equally autochthonous Powers That Be. This is accurate enough to serve the purposes of a polemic or a poetic rant, for they certainly *act* monolithic to those of us who choose not to participate in them, but it is of little help in contending against them. So before we pass on to possible solutions to the problem, we should examine the origins and dynamics of these two—first the Powers That Be and then the Totality.

Of course to have material power and to be one of the Powers That Be are two different conditions. To have material power you simply have to have something valuable that people want badly enough to give money or devotion in exchange for it, and these "somethings" can include crack cocaine and innovative tracts on sorcery as well as Mazdas and Diet Pepsi. But to be one of the Powers That Be (instead of having just some small power), you must be in synch with the political State and its laws and also with the Totality itself—and this brings us to the problem of defining and distinguishing these, so incestuous they have become.

Which is to say, when Capital willingly invests its value in media exposure, political influence, and apparent conformity with the legal system, the holders and/or servants of that Capital may count themselves as among the Powers That Are. Money buys the guns that political power grows out of; media providers sell the exposure one needs to make a spot both in the marketplace and in the culture at large; conformity to law and a willingness to pay for guidance through all its arcane twists and turns, as well as to use your cash to influence its content, show the serious nature of your bid to be a player. So you have to be big to be viable, which means you must either serve a massive corporation or be closely allied with one. And to do that you must enter a condition of "limited liability," meaning no responsibility, meaning crippled in spirit and certainly without magickal power. And to defend your position of irresponsible privilege you must use your advertising dollars to support a Totality that works unceasingly to reduce all desire to the will to consume—all physical wants addressed and nothing of spirit remaining to distract from complete corporeal rapport.

But since it is the creation of the Powers That Be, the Totality can hardly be more monolithic than they, and since they aren't, it isn't, really. It's more a common endpoint, as if these Powers groped and stumbled to fill a common need and the Totality was the uniform product of their fumbling—survival of what was most fit to the market, and all that. Its creation was a step-by-step process, with the early stages best categorized as mere "journalism," until technical improvements gave it the raw psychological power needed to supplant the obsolescent spiritual mesocosm.

This is clear enough if we examine the Totality's pre-history as journalism. For centuries the only Media vehicle was the printed page—cheap to produce with or without advertisement, easy to not read, and thus easy for the disinterested citizen to avoid unwanted rapport with the texts it carried. Even when infant television was introduced, there was little hint that it would mature into the cultural Moloch that confronts us today. Witness the so-called "Golden Age of Television," when the networks provided cutting-edge live theater, *Twilight Zone* pushing the cultural parameters and perimeters, or so they say, anyway—I wasn't allowed to stay up late back then. In any case, it did not have the polish then that it does now, and nowhere near the arrogance. But then the flash and dazzle became easier to produce, the cultural revolution of the 60's loosened up sexual display, musicians developed more effective rhythms for manipulating subtle states, and so all of these—visuals, sex and aural intensification—became available to commerce to better sell soap, and put people in a mind to buy it.

But to attain the credibility it needed to take on the role of mesocosm, the Totality had to be more than a glimmering, glamorous billboard. It also needed to address the real world in ways that engendered significant consequence. This it accomplished through its political victories in the 60's and 70's, especially those involving the Civil Rights movement, the Vietnam War, and Watergate—when the Media essentially brought down the government in a constitutional coup. With these triumphs their influence coalesced into a Totality that is now a veritable co-state. It is about as *demo*-cratic as the elected government, simply because unless it pays attention to the *demo*-graphics, it can't give good service to advertisers. Of course the same considerations apply to the creative content that gets put between the ads, bringing us the well-known "lowest common denominator." And good service to advertisers has become all the more important as these corporations turn all the more faceless, ever less creatures of the community, all the more just machines to make money without the encumbrance of members.

Some readers may counter that this Totality I describe is but a poor thing, easy enough to avoid if you can switch off the tube and skim over the lies they print on paper. These readers might agree that my accusations are true enough when applied to the commercial media, which basically sell to advertisers rather than readers and viewers, but has little to do with music, film, published books, works of art and so on, where the consumer buys the text with money instead of sufferance and time. But then the same music and art that can inspire great thoughts or the desire to boogie can be applied to sell soap. And groundbreaking film introduces striking visual imagery and effects that lesser film can use to sell Mazdas. And characters in successful films will be mimicked soon enough on TV. Besides, the publishers and broadcasters and film studios have all come to be owned by the same corporations—rivals, to be sure, but all playing the game by the same rules to manufacture the Grand Simulacrum.

To sum up, then, we can describe the Totality as an organic growth out of Capital. It is "organic" because it is a natural development out of journalism, but a growth that has become a neoplasm to shove aside and replace that old mesocosm that once inculcated spirit into human culture. It is a particularly malignant mutation, to be sure, but still no contrivance, the result of no conspiracy or even any real plan. It's just a tool that the managers of Capital discovered to be useful for moving both product and maintaining cultural and political control. Where once Big Money threw its weight around by raising armies or bribing royal favorites, now it buys influence through a medium that provides the helpful side-effect of alienating the viewer from all opportunities for independent, immediate action. But for this alienating effect to work, the viewer has to be convinced that what is most current, most exciting, *hippest* in life will be found on the tube. And so the cameras crisscross the land, looking for anything vibrant that will stand still while they frame it, film it, edit it, and suck it dry—this so all humanity can be held down on their couches, sold soap, and deluded into thinking that they can actually *do* something besides eat, sleep, and go to work. And if the cameras see anything that acts counter to the interests of the Totality and the Powers That Be, then they will peer all the more closely until the talking heads pass judgment—either to consign this strangeness to Media Oblivion or else to demonize it so the "public" will demand that the Law take action, lest the fabric of society be imperiled.

A close examination of tactics is necessary.

V. On Our Duties as Citizens of the Terminal State

As we consider the actions we might take against the Totality, the Powers That Be, and the Civil State whose guns support them, we would do well to recall the dual principle of Austin Osman Spare. To wit: whenever you define some position as Truth, and defend it as such, you make its opposite necessary and you energize that opposite to the extent of your original assertion. Newton's Third Law also affirms that the quantity of force we use to push outwards is equal to the quantity of force we must absorb. Thus if we address the State or the Powers That Be with force, we cause them to grow more forceful in response.

This is not an admonition to non-violence in any absolute sense, but more a matter of tactical discretion. Non-violence as an ideal is not suited to sorcery, certainly not to Thelema, and even if it were, it would do us little good. The State is set to crush any who oppose its essence, whether this opposition be violent or otherwise. But violence as a strategy calls too much attention to those who would use it, and destroys the Silence necessary for effective magick. Thus peaceful behavior serves more as a camouflage than as any sort of ethical imperative. To keep from being recognized we must be subtle in our work and only strike where they aren't looking, in vulnerable spots they don't even know they have.

Hakim Bey shows himself in general agreement with these considerations with his two main strategies for action: Poetic Terrorism and the Temporary Autonomous Zone, or TAZ.

Poetic Terrorism consists of unexpected, unauthorized art in public places—either in the form of artifact or performance—this art intending to shock, enlighten, dazzle, and generally breach the world-views of those who encounter it before the minions of the Powers That Be recognize it and take it away. "The best PT is against the law, but don't get caught. Art as crime; crime as art," Bey summed up in the *Broadsheet* entitled "Poetic Terrorism." From the same *Broadsheet*:

> Weird dancing in all-night computer banking lobbies. Unauthorized pyrotechnic displays. Land art, earth-works as bizarre alien artifacts strewn in State Parks. Burglarize houses, but instead of stealing, leave Poetic Terrorist objects. Kidnap someone and make them happy.
>
>   Graffiti-art loaned some grace to ugly subways and rigid public monuments—PT art can also be created for public places: poems scrawled in courthouse lavatories, small fetishes abandoned in parks & restaurants, Xerox-art under windshield wipers of parked cars, Big Character Posters pasted on playground walls, anonymous letters mailed to random or chosen recipients (mail fraud), pirate radio transmissions, wet cement.

The audience reaction or aesthetic shock produced by PT ought to be at least as strong as the emotion of terror—powerful disgust, sexual arousal, superstitious awe, sudden intuitive breakthrough, dada-esque angst—no matter whether PT is aimed at one person or at many, no matter whether it is "signed" or anonymous, if it does not change someone's life (aside from the artist) it fails.

Other sorts of direct action that Bey recommends include unusual sexualities and pornopropaganda—also designed to breach conventional views of reality. From the *Broadsheet* entitled "Amour Fou": "in the masturbation of a child it finds concealed (like a Japanese-paper-flower-pill) the image of the crumbling of the State."

So Bey's assault on the State is indirect to an extreme. He attacks by way of the subconscious minds of the citizenry—"subconscious" in its most technical sense, since that last line could have been right out of Wilhelm Reich, if Reich had been a poet.

But Bey is not so foolish that he presumes that the individuals thus enlightened can then attack the Terminal State one-on-one. Nor does he propose uniting to attack. His strategy is more one of uniting to evade. For this he suggests using the "Temporary Autonomous Zone," or TAZ. In his essay of the same name, Bey makes no claim of inventing the TAZ. Nor does he go so far as to define it, preferring to cite instances ranging from the Assassins of Hassan-i Sabbah to Caribbean pirate enclaves of the 17th century to the modern carnivals and communes like Mardi Gras and the festive markets that used to follow Grateful Dead shows. It is a space outside the political map, a space that cannot be "mapped." "Metaphorically it unfolds within the fractal dimensions invisible to the cartography of Control." Bey compares the TAZ to the insurgency, the revolutions that history defines as failures because they do not last, and thus do not follow the standard political sequence of revolt, reaction, betrayal and repression. It is a rejection of State power that avoids State power by figuratively running between its legs, then vanishing.

The "Temporary" in TAZ is its defining characteristic, its opening to grace, and also its limitation. It is fleeting, so it doesn't tend to attract the torpid gaze of the status quo. Bey tells us that its greatest strength is in its defiance of normal categories of Being:

> ...the State cannot recognize it because history has no definition of it. As soon as the TAZ is named (represented, mediated), it must vanish, it will vanish, leaving behind it an empty husk, only to spring up again somewhere else, once again invisible because undefinable in terms of the Spectacle. The TAZ is thus a perfect tactic for an era in which the State is omnipresent and all-powerful and yet simultaneously riddled with cracks and vacancies.

History cannot recognize the TAZ because history describes what states do in time. By their willingness to step into the moment and out of time, the members of each Zone put themselves at 90° to the historical dimension. The TAZ must vanish at the point of its definition in history. If anyone attempts to re-present it in such a way that it may be mediated, it risks absorption by the Totality and consequent emasculation. In the event that they find themselves being textualized and mediated, the members of a true TAZ will end their association at once, or in any case cause it to dissolve and reform in a new context.

The TAZ is an encampment of guerrilla ontologists: strike and run away. Keep moving the entire tribe, even if it's only data on the Web. The TAZ must be capable of defense, but both the "strike" and the "defense" should, if possible, evade the violence of the State, which is no longer a meaningful violence. The strike is made at structures of control, essentially at ideas; the defense is "invisibility," a martial art, and "invulnerability"—an "occult" art within the martial arts. The nomadic war machine conquers without being noticed and moves on before the map can be adjusted.

Of course the "T" in TAZ is also its greatest limitation. It is a peak experience for the individuals involved but, as Bey admits, too *temporary* to change the world. After any given TAZ dissolves, the Totality remains to absorb its husk so it might use any vestigial power to update and vitalize its own shimmering façade. Witness what happened after the Deadheads' nomadic culture had been effectively shut down—a suppression carried out by the Grateful Dead itself, to a significant extent, under threat of being banned from all their venues. All of the sudden the band became commercially acceptable, with tie-dyed fashions everywhere, the band contributing show footage to PBS fundraisers, senators and even Presidents lauding their virtues and gently chiding them over the liberties they took with the Law. The insurgency was over. What power the rebels were unable to absorb was taken over by the Totality to vitalize its façade of hipness. Garcia's death was just the last nail in the coffin. And now you hardly hear the music anymore, unless you play it yourself.

Of course a major problem with the Deadhead phenomenon was its size. The band went along in happy semi-obscurity until 1987, when their album *In the Dark* came out, with the hit "Touch of Gray," and suddenly there were just too many people who couldn't get tickets hanging around outside. Thus what had once been a backwater in American culture became "news"; the gaze of the Totality fixed hard upon them; and the State responded with all the tools at its disposal. These were legion, indeed, since the Deadheads were America's most coherent opposition to the "War on Drugs" and so the whole phalanx of guns and law could be brought down hard upon them.

Bey makes this point in his essay "Permanent TAZs," where he includes the Deadheads with "MOVE in Philadelphia, the Koreshites of Waco,...Rainbow Tribes, computer hackers, squatters, etc.," who "have been targeted for varying intensity levels of extermination." But Bey notes that there are other groups that seem to get by well enough, and proposes two factors that might be relevant: avoidance of publicity and closed access.

Avoidance of publicity is, of course, the avoidance of consumption by the Totality, even if only its local sub-branches. To be given "news coverage" in any form is to be confined as text within a commercial context. And as if being turned into a text—pixels on a screen, squiggly lines on paper—isn't bad enough, those who so textualize you will be less concerned with presenting an accurate picture in a relevant context than with getting consumers to gaze upon the spaces between the ads. Entertainment value is the supreme criterion. But once you're in the public record, no matter what distortions that record includes, that is a brush stroke in your media caricature. And to be so characterized by the Totality is like having it insert a valve within you so it might draw your power whenever it needs it to refresh its glamour.

Access is a more personal question. Bey observes that "'open-membership' communes inevitably end up swamped with freeloaders and sex-starved pathetic creeps." So a "Permanent Autonomous Zone" has to be able to choose its members, which of course involves all sorts of messy politics, as anyone with experience with occult orders well knows. But closed membership gives one the option of excluding the sorts of people who want to see themselves on television, thus avoiding the publicity that makes coherent work within the group impossible to sustain.

This brings us to an unpleasant fact of modern life, that quite apart from its primal will to self-preservation, the State exists because there is a demand for its services. There are people who covet, people who rage, people who lust and impregnate and have no care for the new life that ensues. So the State is necessary to keep order within the society wherein these people reside, and we would be starry-eyed indeed if we thought we could simply do away with it. Nor need it necessarily restrict us as we pursue our essential purposes.

To the contrary, as the vestiges of obsolete mesocosmic order continue to deteriorate, the State will find itself ever more preoccupied with mere reactive attempts to keep civil peace. This will leave open vast reaches of cultural space for those affinity groups capable of avoiding institutional attention, even as they maintain coherence among themselves. Within each such space a unique mesocosm could evolve, one devoted to the spiritual perpetuation of the affinity group in that space. And so could a new cultural landscape emerge, but only visible to those who can look askance, and catch it on its edge.

So I think a possible solution would be the evolution of a parallel society made up of loosely linked Autonomous Zones acting surreptitiously in the midst of the status quo, but not of it. Now since any affinity group—from a hippy commune to platoon of soldiers—works best if everyone in it knows everyone else, each Zone must necessarily be limited in size. But individual zones—call them pods—can be affiliated with larger aggregations, like congregations within a religious denomination. Details like private vs. community property, community vs. public education, community vs. individual economic endeavors, requirements for entry into the group and individual responsibilities to it could all be left up to the separate pods, as would the type of camouflage each chose as a means to conceal its true nature from the profane. The only requirement for inclusion into the larger whole must be the avoidance of all publicity.

And yet survival as a group and prosperity for its members would probably necessitate one other common characteristic: the invention/evolution of a group cult—that is, the design of a unique rite to focus the spiritual energies of the group's members in such a way that the group is preserved and life within it is enhanced. Such a cult would be a religion for the group alone, a tool for redirecting the members' interests from "the cravings of desire and ambition" to "the divinity within them." And of course the prime tool for inventing effective cults, fetishes, and pagan rites in general is sorcery. Though presently it might be best known as a way for individuals to do their wills, it could also help generate the mythic and ritual content needed for a pod-sized Mystery, an initiation for which only the pod's members would be worthy. And compatible Mysteries could be one basis for formalizing affiliations among independent pods.

It would seem advisable for the technique of sorcery *as such* to be included as part of the initiatory curriculum for any pod's cult. For one thing, it would help keep all members on an equal psychic footing, ensuring that the organic pagan *cultus* does not degenerate into a "cult" in the pejorative modern sense—that is, a bunch of psychomanipulated devotees exploited by their sociopathic guru. By educating the youth in the techniques of magick, they would each learn to become aware if such a technique were being used on them. Also, by encouraging competence in ritual magick, the group would ensure a perpetual development of liturgical innovation. With sorcerous techniques, passions and rivalries could be self-modified before they degenerated into such extremes of greed, rut or rage that they called the State down upon them. And competence in the use of the subtle body serves to generate the personal power necessary to carry out these purposes and also maintain and enhance personal health.

It could be suggested that rapport with the ecosystem was the archetypal tribal "faith," and that devotion to a divinely-instituted hierarchy was the "faith" of civilization. In our post-civitas time, then, we must invent a new way of praising the Lord. It would seem as if a custom of magickally-competent pod-cults could give great latitude to individual practice even as it provided a forum for the group to act according to a common magickal purpose. A further point in magick's favor is that sorcerous union is something that comes easier by way of the pod than through the familial hierarchy upon which civilization is based. In his essay "The Temporary Autonomous Zone," Hakim Bey addresses the family/TAZ dichotomy thusly:

> The nuclear family is the base unit of consensus society, but not of the TAZ... The nuclear family, with its attendant "oedipal miseries," appears to have been a Neolithic invention, a response to the "agricultural revolution" with its imposed scarcity and imposed hierarchy. The Paleolithic model is at once more primal and more radical: the band. The typical hunter/gatherer nomadic or semi-nomadic band consists of about 50 people. Within larger tribal societies the band structure is fulfilled by clans within the tribe, or by sodalities such as initiatic or secret societies, hunt or war societies, "children's republics," and so on. If the nuclear family was produced by scarcity (and results in miserliness), the band is produced by abundance—and results in prodigality. The

family is closed, by genetics, by the male's possession of women and children, by the hierarchic totality of agricultural/industrial society. The band is open—not to everyone, of course, but to the affinity group, the initiates sworn to a bond of love. The band is not part of the larger hierarchy, but rather part of a horizontal pattern of custom, extended kinship, contract and alliance, spiritual affinities, etc.

The high time of the Paleolithic was when mastodons roamed the earth, and it lasted until our ancestors ate them all. With that it became necessary to develop ever more precise technology to kill the ever smaller, quicker animals that were left after such big game had been hunted out. And then domestication was invented, and agriculture, and so there we were, pushed by scarcity into digging dirt. But we kept on with the technology, so here we are again, our machines bringing us a new abundance. But it's a twisted sort of abundance, where you can either have it all but have no life left over, or have a life but be obliged to get by with very little. Band-like PAZ-pods could provide individuals ways to unite against the blind mechanism of markets, perhaps even letting them take of the economy's abundance without risk to their souls. The band united in works of magick would be a significant foe, worthy of sincere efforts at reconciliation. The band as a collective resource for the nurturing, education and sorcerous training of children is a potential treasure trove. The band as a generator of unique realities is a possibility not yet tapped, but perhaps precursor to a time when Reality becomes arbitrary, truly a matter of power more than substance.

We needn't worry that we guerrilla ontologists seem too few in number to bring on the orderly dismemberment of the Terminal State, which even now crumbles around us, certainties falling from its façade like so many fractured cornices and dislodged medallia. The political powerscape is entering a chaotic phase. The old dynamic is no longer able to transmit efficiently the power it must move if it is to fulfill its function. The backed-up power seeks an outlet, and if some obscure alternative is able to do a better job with it than the old standard, then it will grow exponentially until the old dynamic has been entirely replaced.

For the past 5000 years, "civilization" was the most efficient way to focus energy to support human life. Like the flow of a mighty river, it was not a dynamic that anyone could resist for long. One simply went along, riding with the current on mesocosmic rafts. And then came the industrial revolution, and the invention of speedboats, though most people are lucky if they can afford a two-cycle outboard. But rivers silt up, and then break out in new, faster courses, and then even a 400-horse inboard won't take you where you used to go. Civilization has silted up. The press of technology and its attendant social stress has backed up the human flow to where it can no longer remain within its banks. Any new channel that is potentially more efficient need only make itself available; the pressure of circumstances will seek it out and turn it from a trickle into a flood in a twinkling, if the State does not see it first and block it off. This blocking has happened often enough before; the levees are high on both banks and the delta extends far into the sea from all the times the State has seen social innovation and damned it up before a new channel could establish itself. But that just makes the short-cut to the sea all the steeper, all the more compelling to the human flow so very sick of arrogant stagnation.

Lurk!

Rising Through The Decline

A Magickal Look at Oswald Spengler

I. The Current Situation

The World Corporate Order reigns supreme on the face of the earth.

The full force of Pax Americana stands ready to defend the laws of its commercial custom.

The shimmering glamour of the Media Totality works unceasingly to convince us that this custom is simply the way things are, that the reality it imposes is the only one any sane person could possibly recognize.

Undisputed victor in the 20th century's "Wars between Contending States," and sufficiently self-aware to realize that the business of America *is* business, the United States Government placed no heavy burdens on its defeated foes, and thus no tiresome obligations on its friends and allies. Its only demand was acquiescence to a way of doing business, an assimilation of Anglo-American commercial practice, corporate structure, and values of free trade, open currency and unrestricted movement of capital. Once that form has been taken on, no government can become overtly unruly, for all will in practice be subservient to the market—transnational, fleshless, wholly abstract governor of the whole affair, in the best Darwinian tradition.

Capital waits, a jewelry store left suspiciously unlocked, a tree, burdened with fruit, surrounded by quicksand. Over time capital infiltrates, and then absorbs, and by its digestion all that passes through it turns non-human—units of equity and debt that must always be (for a small commission) freely interchangeable with all other units of equity and debt, the several varieties of cash, and even those metals that still retain an aura of monetization. (Dream of forgotten Blood, eventually to awake!) But all must be valued as if they were equivalent, the proportions between them under constant adjustment by the blind hand of the market, ultimate judge of all commercial fact.

Acceptance of this dynamic as the Way of All Things is the price of admission to the World Corporate Order, most certain avenue to wealth in the new millennium. Once any human enterprise, institution or individual has been thus co-opted, it becomes just another nexus of action/reaction wired into this planet-girdling brain. Each becomes a neuron in a multi-dimensional, giganodical network whose action is the omnipresent dialectic of supply and demand, fear and greed, hope and need, each impulse digitized and processed at light speed to collectively manifest as shimmering fluctuations in the globe-spanning field that is money. All are welcome to abandon self to this disensouling embrace, encouraged to take of its bounty regardless of race, creed or country of national origin, or rather to the exclusion of these, for capital knows nothing of them. To truly enter rapport with capital, one must live in a state—both mental and political—whose frontiers are transparent to capital's movements, and thus available for transformation on capital's terms. Acquiescence to this state connects one to the source of all wealth and power, this at the price of the sure loss of any special Destiny.

Destiny is the one coin the market cannot convert. The World Corporate Order turns Destiny to lead.

II. Danilevsky and Spengler

The first need for those who would oppose the World Corporate Order is a strategy for pursuing this opposition that harmoniously combines personal survival with revolutionary effectiveness. For this we must look at the problem from the widest possible perspective. Many esotericists of all beliefs, working assumptions and techniques have asserted that this Babylon must fall, and it certainly seems to be accelerating toward some end point, crisis point, or phase of transformation. Simply because it is growing so quickly, it must soon collapse in upon itself, or else launch itself to the stars.

Of course for every culture up until now, decline has been the rule, so it's easy to suppose that a similar sort of collapse will eventually assault the System as it stands today. On the other hand it is possible that the industrial revolution has changed everything, creating a civilization with the momentum to transcend the usual pattern of rise and fall. But then we can also see industrialization as merely a characteristic feature of Western culture, and no reason why it should be any more immortal than any other. Rome fell. Egypt and Babylon are buried in the earth. Each of these also had some special claim to unique status, but it couldn't save them in the end. Perhaps industrialization has even made the West more susceptible to collapse, just as connoisseurs of methamphetamines are not known for their longevity. So for the purposes of this essay, I will assume that what goes up must come down. To explore the historical ramifications of this postulate, I will have recourse to two very similar models of cultural evolution, models which (when applied to the situation of the West) are generally called "pessimistic" because they make it very clear that we are approaching an apogee of some sort right now, and thus a decline must follow.

Cyclical historical models were common in the ancient world, but in the post-Enlightenment West two theorists stand out: the Russian Nikolai Danilevsky (1822–1885) and the German Oswald Spengler (1880–1936). Neither of these men was by profession an academic historian. Instead they sought to discover in history pragmatic strategies and tools to use to promote their specific political objectives. Though the politics of Danilevsky and Spengler were to be in opposition through two world wars and the cold one that followed, both men developed remarkably similar understandings of the way cultures are born and die.

Nikolai Danilevsky was educated as a botanist and made a career in the Czarist civil service, eventually becoming commissioner of fisheries. He wrote extensively on various historical and economic topics, but the book that brings him to our attention is *Russia and Europe*, first serialized in the journal *Zara* in 1869. Basically, it is wide-ranging analysis of cultural evolution that attempts to answer the question: why does Europe hate Russia and resist so strenuously all attempts by Russia to encourage any sort of pan-Slavic union?

Oswald Spengler's university training was also in the natural sciences, though he had a strong interest in the classics and did his doctoral work on Heraclitus. Upon graduation he began a career as a high school teacher, earning the high regard of both students and colleagues, but in 1911 he resigned to pursue his destiny as an independent scholar. The first volume of his study was published in July of 1918, a month before the German Army's collapse on the Western Front, a significant portent considering both the intent and the title of his great work. *The Decline of the West* is a wide-ranging analysis of cultural evolution that seeks to advance an almost unstated agenda (which remains unspecified until the end of the second volume, published in 1922): the victory of the Prussian values of organic culture, with rank awarded according to the extent of one's duties to society, over the cut-throat culture of the Anglo-Americans, where rank is awarded according to one's success in economic competition. Spengler saw World War I as the first scene in the last act of this struggle. He sought to inspire the German people to a last, brief return to old virtue so they might triumph in the Final Conflict to Come, and thus rule instead of serve in the centuries of ever more corrupt empire that must inevitably follow.

Despite their opposing political agendas, Danilevsky and Spengler both developed very similar models of what cultures in general tend to do, and made similar predictions for what is in store for the West. Both men saw cultures as discrete multinational social organisms with life spans of about one thousand years, but mortal nonetheless, each following a characteristic life-cycle that makes its behavior at any given stage more or less predictable. And both men agreed that the West was well into its phase of late maturity, and only has the stiffening of a long senescence to look forward to. For Danilevsky this was the reason Europe repressed young Russia and worked to thwart any tendency toward pan-Slavic cohesion; he felt that Europe had an intuitive certainty that if the Slavs gained a critical mass, they would spawn a distinct, new culture that would overwhelm the doddering West. For Spengler, this was the reason that his was the time of total war that it was, the West being then well into the phase where the nations of any culture struggle one against the other until the strongest attains preeminence.

Ironically, the political programs promoted by both Danilevsky and Spengler failed miserably. Seventy years of Communist suffocation has driven western Slavdom into the arms of the West and crippled the eastern economically. And though Germany was able to conjure enough old discipline to terrify its neighbors in the final act of the "Wars between Contending States," it did so by abandoning itself to a charismatic madman who empowered himself with hate—hate over all—even to the extent of abandoning sound strategy, throwing away political and military victory, and disregarding the survival of the nation in order to satisfy it. And yet Spengler's historical model continues on track. Pax Americana has taken on the imperial roll that Spengler's model reserves for the victor, though its hand is light since it is the market that really controls, the carrot rather than the stick, political power growing out of a tub of butter.

And the only price for dipping in is everything you really are.

According to Danilevsky and Spengler, then, the Western adventure is complete. Western civilization is doomed to an indefinite continuation of the present decline, with a progressive coarsening of all its features: commerce, government, quality of life, the arts. Even so, it will remain invulnerable to any sort of human violence—whether from Asia or Islam or from rebellion from within—until several more centuries have passed. But then this need not inhibit those of us who would establish something new. We need not fight against this stagnating anachronism; it is already falling in on itself as quickly as it can. Instead we need to be aware of Pax Americana's somewhat unintended fertility. Which is to say, the stagnation of the Old provides a rich field for the germination of the New. An understanding of the dynamics that initiate and support such germinations could help us exploit this circumstance, and bring success to our purposes.

III. Models of Culture

Nikolai Danilevsky and Oswald Spengler formulated models of cultural evolution that agree on all major points. Both saw cultures as the main engines of historical development; both had similar notions of which historical entities have constituted cultures thus far in history—and hence the relative size or significance required for an historical entity to earn the designation "culture." For Danilevsky there were ten of these: the Egyptian, the Chinese, the Assyrio-Babylonian-Phoenician-Chaldean-Ancient Semitic, the Hindu, the Iranian, the Hebrew, the Greek, the Roman, the Neo-Semitic-Arabian, and the Germano-Romantic or European. To these he added the Aztec and the Incan, murdered by Spain before they could pass out of adolescence.

For Spengler there have been about eight cultures so far: the Egyptian, the Chinese, the Babylonian, the Indian, the Classical (Greece, Macedonia, Rome), the Magian (Byzantine, Persian, Jewish, Arab, Ottoman), the Western or "Faustian" (Western Europe and North America), and the Aztec, which Spengler also saw as having been murdered.

Both men treated these cultures as individuals with more or less uniform life-cycles—about a thousand years. There is a progression from youth to vigorous maturity to decline, and then an entry into an old age of indefinite duration that both men designated "civilization." Civilization is the "historyless" condition of stasis that endures after the culture has accomplished its Destiny and thus exhausted its sense of purpose. Such a condition may last a few centuries, until the civilization has degenerated to the extent that it is vulnerable to external scourges, as was the Roman to the Goths and Huns. Or a civilization can endure for millennia if history and geography conspire to protect the fragile artifact, as was the case with ancient Egypt.

The immense value of Danilevsky and Spengler's work is the ability of their models to predict the behavior of a culture once its stage of development has been determined, simply because every culture passes through the same stages in its progress toward civilization, and exhibits similar behavior at each stage. This behavior will dominate areas ranging from politics to aesthetics, economics to the art of war. Thus (taking Spengler's choice of cultures), the Classical produced Alexander at about the same stage of life—middle age—that the West produced Napoleon, and in each case this inaugurated two centuries of war to determine final supremacy: Roman and American, respectively. The same could be said for the Magian (which in Spengler's view was brought to birth in the midst of the Classical around the year One), with wars between Byzantium, Persia and Arabia finally culminating in Ottoman dominion over the entire middle east.

That the West is now in transition from vital culture to stiffening civilization should be clear to anyone without a cyborg link to the media feed. The United States of America may have won the Wars between Contending States, but now it must endure the rather less inspiring process of becoming an empire at home as well as abroad. We will examine in Part VIII Spengler's take on how such degeneration might proceed.

Other areas of agreement between Danilevsky and Spengler include the following: 1) the nations within a culture will all share similar languages, modes of perception, and aesthetic imperatives—in other words, their citizens will be able to understand one another with little difficulty; 2) most of the events making up these nations' histories will involve interactions with one another, rather than with the nations of any alien cultures; 3) the underlying premises behind a culture's way of understanding reality and acting in it will be beyond the experience of the members of other cultures, and these premises may not be assimilated by them; and 4) cultures can only enjoy healthy growth and development when they are free from political domination from the outside.

The differences between Danilevsky and Spengler have more to do with the two men's temperaments than any fundamental theoretical disagreements. Danilevsky, by profession a natural scientist and administrator, was much more analytical. Spengler, on the other hand, was more intuitive. Even when he was back in his teaching days, that was how his students described his style of lecturing, and they also reported that he was able to maintain strict order in his classroom without resort to harsh penalties, indicating that he was able to carry this into his personal interactions as well. Thus while Danilevsky confessed himself ignorant of the dynamics driving cultures from birth to senile decay, Spengler had the insight to discern a mechanism that I personally find to be exceptionally penetrating.

Spengler's main weak point was his tendency to take his intuitive visions for fundamental laws, ignoring even those exceptions that only complicate his model, rather than contradict it. An example would be his refusal to entertain pseudomorphosis (see Part V) as a positive alternative to collapse. Danilevsky's main weakness lies in what I see as his erroneous identification of the cultures that have thus far played their part in the world. For instance he separates the Roman from the Greek, while Spengler simply has Rome winning the rule over Classical civilization from all the other states in the Hellenistic Mediterranean. Also, Danilevsky sees Byzantine culture as a final stagnation of the Roman, while Spengler quite nicely integrates it with the Jewish, Persian and Arabian into what he calls the Magian.

Since in order to make use of this model we need to settle on just which cultures did exist, in the sections to come I will be using Spengler as my primary inspiration, while Danilevsky waits to supplement the more limited aspects of Spengler's treatment. This will allow me to present Spengler's intuitive vision of cultural dynamics without interruption, all the more essential since these dynamics seem quite amenable to magickal interpretation.

Magick, as I will use the term here, is a psychic technology. Though the subject as a whole may be seen as one of bewildering complexity—so much so that it is customarily referred to as "the occult"—most of this complexity vanishes once we realize that there is an invisible *stuff* within and around us, a power that animates all consciousness, a stuff that might most conveniently be called "psychic energy." When it occupies an animal or plant, it acts as the energy that animates that organism's awareness, and here it is entirely subjective. This is psychic energy's "normal" mode, but we may also regard it as objective so as to manipulate it to promote our purposes. The specific subroutines it follows within our unconscious minds may be treated as "spirits" that we may control through magickal techniques under the authority of our wills. Its channels through the body may be identified and made more definite, and its flow through these enhanced and optimized for the benefit of personal prowess and physical health. It may even be split off from consciousness to act independently, and then it can produce events and insights that have been called "paranormal." What actually happens in such cases depends on the cause of the split. If it results from the repression of an unpleasant fact, the energy may discharge as an omen, a 'coincidental' event that displays a symbolic analogue of the fact thus ignored. On the other hand, a magician can conjure "energized enthusiasm" and intentionally focus it into a talisman, thus splitting psychic energy off into a magickally effective container that can carry the power to a specific place or time. If all goes according to plan, the energy will then discharge as an event or inspiration that can help the sorcerer accomplish his or her purposes.

Magick has been ubiquitous throughout human history and prehistory. Born in shamanism and an element within any effective religion, it has played a role in the development of every high culture that has thus far appeared on the earth. Even so, in the past the exploitation of psychic energy has always been kept in the background while the more solid aspects of human life were mastered. Now the mastery of these solid aspects is complete, and the realm of psyche stands before us as an undiscovered country open to conquest. At the present time the Powers That Be in the West consider the occult arts to be beneath their contempt, holding psychic energy at arm's length by defining it as "subjective," and thus "unscientific." This is their fundamental error, a blind spot so deep that it festers as if it were an abscess. Any civilization will be materialistic, but the Faustian surpasses all previous limits. Its whole imagination has been devoted to the techniques of forcing matter to conform to will. Thus the potentates of the West have no inkling that the energy that animates imagination, passion and all other aspects of consciousness may itself be applied to the actualization of event. To apply magick to the purposes of culture is to occupy a ground that is beyond the horizons of the Lords of Civilization, and yet one that lies directly adjacent to their realm. It is a territory we dare not leave unoccupied.

IV. Blood, Intellect, Destiny in Space

For Spengler the engine that forges culture and drives its evolution from birth to senescence is the dialectic between Blood and Intellect.

Now let me here emphasize that in using the word "Blood," Spengler was not promoting ideas of "genetic purity" or "breeding" or any of that other racist tripe. Instead he saw Blood simply as life force, making his take on it more in line with Yahweh's, who had this to say about it:

> Only be sure that thou eat not the blood: for the blood is the life; and thou mayst not eat the life with the flesh.
> Thou shalt not eat it; thou shalt pour it upon the earth as water.
> Thou shalt not eat it; that it may go well with thee, and with thy children after thee, when thou shalt do that which is right in the sight of the Lord. (Deut. 12:23–25)

Which makes this one of the first shots in the war between immanence and transcendence, and we all know where Yahweh stands in that contest.

Be all that as it may, the Blood is the life, and life lives in both time and in space. Time is inescapable, the medium of both Blood and life, and as such may be pushed into the background of awareness. But to act in space—to move into it and through it—requires purpose and entails risk, and each movement presents a unique risk. Comprehension of this risk requires memory, self-awareness and rational thought—Intellect—as does any sort of strategy for avoiding risk. When primates joined together to address this problem in a cooperative way, the first social culture emerged, and thus the beginning of our long tribal twilight.

This predawn period lasted for dozens of millennia. Though neither Danilevsky nor Spengler would have denied it consideration as culture, it was not what they called high culture, and it had no tendency to follow the life cycle characteristic of high cultures, being capable of persisting for as long as the natural environment that supported it. Danilevsky called the cultural artifacts that tribalism produces "ethnographic material," stating that they serve as raw materials that emergent high cultures may assemble to build their grand edifices. He added that when civilizations finally disintegrate, their populations fall back into this condition until the next high culture incorporates their cultural artifacts into its New Thing.

The urge to culture is fear and awe of death, which Spengler saw as analogous to *depth*, the *space* that pulls life into itself and swallows, sucking Blood in through its vortex of want. Awareness of the inevitability of one's own death was the first act of abstract Intellection, and it is in defiance of death that Intellect disciplines Blood so they together form culture—a worthy tool for managing depth, however it may be conceived. When space was the inalterable natural environment, Intellect confined itself to the dynamics of family, clan and the natural world, and the result was the tribal twilight. But when Intellect made the leap of assigning some special quality or purpose to space, and then organized Blood to exploit that quality or advance that purpose, that is when high culture began.

When space can be given a form, it is no longer a vortex that swallows Blood, but instead becomes a fertile environment that will return wealth and sustain life. Organization allows for the orderly extension of Blood in space, permitting the exploitation of the environment and consequent productive flair that characterizes high culture. The progression of this effort from bold quest to total control marks the culture's maturation from youth to old age. And when this progress is over and the space's form is fixed, culture is finished as well, and only the stiffening civilization remains.

According to Spengler, the impetus for this organization will be from the land, from those people who recognize this special form and work to cultivate conformity to it as a discipline. Historically, these people have generally appeared as a landed aristocracy, and Spengler defines this as *the first estate*. By their discipline they distinguish themselves from the mass of the peasantry, and by the success of their discipline do they go on to obtain political supremacy. But this leadership position will not go unchallenged. Be they Christian, pagan, Buddhist or whatever, the clerics of the time—*the second estate*—will oppose their Eternal Holy Truth to the aristocracy's political fact. And because the aristocracy needs Truth as a tool for organization and control, a sort of dialectic ensues, one that tends towards political turmoil, but which at the same time generates the aesthetic complexities of the high culture.

But this dialectic between aristocracy and clergy does not long continue without interference. It is soon complicated by the emergence of a *third estate*, the urban bourgeoisie. The cultural ferment consequent to the interplay between the first two estates makes inevitable the economic activity that requires the services of the third: bankers, merchants, owners of manufactories. As towns grow into cities, these ever more moneyed individuals dispute with aristocracy and clergy for control of the social organism. In so doing they struggle against the very forms that first gave the culture its economic strength, through which they ensure their own wealth. Thus the efforts of the bourgeoisie will be circumspect at first, though as they gain economic power, political influence inevitably comes more easily. After about five centuries (1300–1800 in the West), they will be strong enough to bid for supremacy, which they do by offering full enfranchisement to the urban masses—*the fourth estate*. The merchant princes assume they can manipulate these "masses" with their wealth, and even if the people themselves resist them, the mechanism that selects the ones who write the laws will surely be vulnerable, and there's always the media, whose purchase and correct application can paste a gloss of credibly corrupt normality over the most squalid goings on.

All this is simply to say that the high bourgeoisie establishes democracy as a tool for overthrowing aristocracy and the power of the church, and then corrupts it. But in the process the old cultural forms are rendered largely meaningless—broken, obsolete and no longer capable of preserving the social regularity that once provided an organic sort of control, instead of the contrived control imposed by Intellect. Thus must custom be replaced by law, a substitution that generally occurs about the same time as the culture's conquest of its special form of space. With this the culture's Destiny is accomplished, culture is finished and civilization begun, for there isn't anything very meaningful to do within *that space* anymore.

There only remains the massive contrivance that is the civilization itself, an arrangement of such complexity as to be wholly Intellect, with only the most attenuated flow of Blood capable of pushing through to animate it. This complexity is vital simply to adjust for all the social contradictions that the civilization must reconcile within itself. These contradictions become ever more troublesome as the culture's conquest of its space nears completion, for with this the cultural imperative is accomplished and the need for any unity against adversity disappears. With this focus gone, the principle life-purpose for the citizen of a civilization is to *make money*. There isn't much social cohesion to be found in that, and high complexity in service of directionless indulgence cannot last forever, even if for a time it has the power to rule the world.

Over the run of centuries such self-absorption enervates to the extent that the civilization finally falls prey to whatever Scourge of God rides in from over the horizon to loot its bloated carcass. The surviving remnants will then be left as a fertile ground for the next culture to grow out of, a culture with its own concept of space to organize and exploit, and so will the process begin again.

Spengler believed that each high culture will have its own notion of how space must be perceived, understood and dominated. He felt that each culture's special concept of space was a *prime symbol*, unacknowledged by its members but serving as the source for all the other aspects of the culture's identity: its arts, religion, politics, even its mathematics. This space is the field whereupon the culture will win its Destiny. Its unique topography and the special tools that can master it will inspire the unique approach the culture takes, and the special forms that facilitate it.

According to Spengler, in ancient Egypt the idea of space was the one-dimensional, linear progress from birth through life into death and rebirth in the underworld. Inspired by the linearity of the Nile valley, it was embodied in the architecture of temple and tomb, the processional way leading from gate to altar, the paintings and bas-reliefs all marching toward that holy place, drawing the progress along to the presence of the mummy or god.

For the Classical mind, space was all about the local, the here-and-now, the sensually present. In politics, the city-state was paramount. In art, it was the standing nude and the perfection of the columned temple, rising up shining on a hill. In ethics, the ideal was the cultivation of the individual's body, mind and spirit, the attainment of balanced excellence. Greek mathematics concerned itself with the tuning of the string, the figure drawn in the sand, the temple built of stone. It was all about the measurement of what could be sensed. Its domain was the "natural" numbers; numerical abstraction—including the concept of "zero"—had no reality for it. The gods were worshipped through localized cults satisfying the immediate needs of the worshippers; abstract dogmas were never formulated. The dead were burned and Hades was a place of shadows. Only heroes—those so renowned that they attracted vivifying sacrifices from the living—enjoyed an afterlife in the Elysian Fields.

For the Magian mind, Destiny was worked out in the dogma space defined by the canonical texts of True Religion, bounded by the time between Creation and Apocalypse. Whether Zoroastrian, Jewish, Christian or Moslem, every Magian man or woman was born into a community of the faithful. All were convinced that their own small acts influenced the cosmic struggle between their Creator God and his Primal Opponent, all Magian religion being to some extent dualistic. Membership in the community was ritually established by Baptism or circumcision, and if the member adhered to the Holy Law and worked the Work of the Creator, then both His Enterprise and that of the community would prosper. Politically, this focus on religion could result in theocracy on the one hand, and on the other hand in the accommodation by the State of many orthodoxies, each sure of its own unique connection to Cosmic Truth. In Magian architecture, the dominant form was the dome, the enclosure serving as the embodiment of the dogma space wherein the Cosmic Contest was carried out. And from Diophantes to Omar Khayyam, Magian mathematics was algebraic, a computation of abstract relation rather than measurement of the objects of perception.

For Western or "Faustian" culture, the space wherein Destiny has been confronted and subdued is the three dimensions of physicality—infinite in six directions. Whether the Viking raider/trader sailing across uncharted ocean to engage in commerce and steal loot, the Teutonic knight invading the uncharted steppes to bring feudalism and impose Christianity, or mature European imperialism combining the four and spreading them across the entire planet, the discovery of unknown lands and their subsequent domination and exploitation has been the leitmotif of Faustian culture. Throughout the Faustian centuries—from the eleventh through the twentieth—the architectural expressions of this imperative have emphasized *height*. From the Gothic cathedral to the American skyscraper, the Faustian edifice reaches to the stars. And to facilitate both the Faustian reach and its grasp, the obsession of Western Intellect has always been the discovery and perfection of technics. The Chinese may have invented printing and gunpowder, but for them they remained mere toys for the elite. In the West they became instruments to extend control. From the full-rigged ship to the railroad, from the piston engine to the rocket, from the airplane to the space shuttle, from moveable type to the Internet, Faustian technics has produced the tools the culture needed to ensure that there could be no place anyplace able to escape its embrace. The mathematics of the West is analysis, where the function rules, it being the application of discovered regularity to any contingency. As for religion, there is no transnational community of belief but instead a Church, and the mission of each Church is to more efficiently bring redemption, this cleansing of any moral distraction necessary to permit full concentration on the work of extension. Whether before the battle or before the embarkation, there was always the Eucharist (at least for the first seven centuries or so), casting aside the worst of self so the best could win the day. And for Spengler the art forms most characteristic of the Faustian quest are oil painting, especially the perfection of the science of perspective, followed and superceded by orchestral music, the expression in sound of pure spatial infinity.

This assumption that each culture possesses a unique idea of space is the basis for Spengler's assertion that there can be no meaningful influence between one culture and another, that all the crossbreeding that generates the richness and complexity of a culture comes solely from the interactions between the several nations that make it up. Thus one cannot speak of Athens without reference to Sparta, Delphi and Syracuse; Persia, on the other hand, appears as a barbarous bully whose sole function was to force the Greeks to briefly unite. Then it fell back into the shadows until Alexander imposed a façade of Classical culture upon it, a façade that lasted only a few centuries before the Parthians reasserted cultural self-determination. In the same way, one cannot understand London without Paris, Berlin and—most especially!—Rome, but Moscow is of another world. This of course was Danilevsky's main point, and Spengler was in full agreement. Both men saw Russia as being in a state of cultural birth, and Spengler predicted that its special notion of space will be that of the limitless plane. In his dating he has it just 900 years younger than the West, and so we could assume that it would just now be springing into a vigorous childhood. Perhaps. But then it's possible cultures can commit suicide as well as be murdered.[4] Seventy years of economic totalitarianism is no way to engage in a youthful growth spurt, and one wonders if a child so stunted will be capable of any full-blooded maturity.

More problematic is Spengler's assertion that cultures do not influence their successors. After all, what about Aristotle's domination of Catholic Christianity and early Western science, all those Classical columns on Western buildings, and the fact that every child in America who expects to go to college will try to learn Euclid? Spengler would reply that cultures only take from other cultures what they can apply on their own terms to their own special needs, and all else is discarded. Which is to say, there can be no mingling of Destinies, no contamination of one conception of space by another. Western culture was certainly pushed forward by Aristotle, who demonstrated to the wild tribes of Germans, Franks, Goths and Celts that such high thought was possible. But a great deal of intellectual effort was expended between 1300 and 1700 in the work of getting shut of him. Classical architectural orders may decorate the façades and interiors of Baroque palaces and churches, but more authentic are the frescos on the ceilings they support—mythical and religious figures resting on clouds rising up into the heavens, all painted in perfect perspective, an exquisite complement to the soaring music of a Bach or a Handel. And with regard to mathematics, Spengler makes the point that Descartes' geometry (1637) was not an innovation pushing forward 'traditional' geometry, but "the definitive conception of a new number idea." With Descartes' work geometry was liberated from "servitude to optically-realizable constructions and to measured and measurable lines generally," thus opening the way to "the analysis of the infi-

---

[4] A third sort of premature demise might be accident. It seems that a unique Minoan culture came to be in the bronze age Mediterranean, one which could well have bloomed into full flower had not Thera blown up and essentially crippled it, allowing it to be supplanted by the as-yet-embryonic Classical.

nite." Descartes did not expand on the Euclidean tradition, but overcame it. Instead of lines drawn in the sand and planes one could carve in stone, "there emerged the abstract, spatial, unclassical element of the *point* which was from then on regarded as a group of co-ordered pure numbers." (I: p. 74)

Spengler notes that Western science did its best to emulate the Classical in all things, holding it up as an ideal to be equaled, but in reality each and every effort to do so pushed the West further from it. "The history of Western knowledge is thus one of *progressive emancipation* from Classical thought, an emancipation never willed, but enforced in the depths of the unconscious." (I: p. 76) As Spengler stresses, a culture's idea of space is its prime symbol, one never expressed but lying beneath all the more manifest features that decorate the culture and determine its characteristic behavior. Western consciousness may have seen the Classical as the ideal, but the fundamental Western imperative was to conquer a space that the Classical mind-set shrank from for fear of its unknowable depths. Thus was the West obliged to abandon the Classical in spite of its sincere efforts to preserve it. Today it survives only as an artifact of coins and ruins, etymology and ancient texts. In its totality the Classical remains truly relevant only to antiquarians and historians, and also to those of us who see Western culture becoming just as Bloodless as that of stoa and Caesar. Like the late Roman Republic and early Empire, the culture that was the Faustian has finished its essential journey, even as Faustian civilization rides its momentum in style on towards its inevitable end. Senile, empty of purpose, it will reach a point when it lays open like an overripe fruit to any passing tribe on the look-out for loot. And so will it deteriorate until there is nothing left but remnants—ethnographic material that will be available for assembly into the "Next Thing" when a new people discover a new way to organize space.

But then we need to wonder if a complete collapse is necessary before the Next Thing makes its entrance. Mightn't the New come up in the midst of the Old, its fresh Blood reanimating at least the physical infrastructure of the Old before irreparable decay has set in? The point here is that Spengler did indeed recognize that new cultures could grow up in the midst of still vigorous civilizations, a process he called "historical pseudomorphosis." Though he saw it in a largely negative light, his analysis of its dynamics, and how a new culture defines itself in the midst of a declining civilization, can perhaps help us address our current situation. The World Corporate Order is well on its way to dominating every nook and cranny of the three dimensions of physical space. Quite frankly, the field of Faustian Destiny is becoming quite uninhabitable. Each additional acre of pavement, each regimentation of creativity to the service of profit, each addition to the edifice of law constricts the flow of Blood still more, until the extremities begin to ulcerate and the stench of necrosis becomes unbearable.

Our mission is clear. Unless we can somehow transmigrate the magnificent Faustian edifice into some new space beyond Faustian Destiny, the populace will become too exhausted to carry on the work of maintaining it, and its dissolution will be inevitable. But its construction has so depleted the planet that by the time the Next Thing is born, there will hardly remain sufficient resources to get a replacement started, and never again could our present scale be reached. The edifice Faustian culture has built has put us on the threshold of the stars, but if the culture can't be replaced without wrecking the edifice, our chance of reaching them is gone.

V. Historical Pseudomorphosis

In its original usage "pseudomorphosis" is a term for a geological process. A crystal is encased in rock; the crystal erodes away or dissolves, leaving an empty mold; and the mold is filled by another type of mineral, producing an artifact that takes the *false form* of the original crystal. A more familiar example is petrified wood, where silicates infiltrate the structure of cellulose and lignin, taking on the wood's form even while it decays. Or even cuprified wood. I have in my possession a bronze arrowhead. Along the smoothly forged shank there appears to be a residue of wood, with grain that looks like wood but hard and brittle and blue-green:

copper salts that took the false form of the wood in the arrow shaft, which had rotted away twenty-five centuries before.

For Spengler, historical pseudomorphosis is a process whereby a new culture is placed by circumstances in a geographical area already dominated by either a stronger culture or a still-vigorous civilization. The old form is too strong to be broken, so instead the new culture grows up inside the old until it finally rots away. Thus the New is forced to take the superficial shape of the Old, even as it is driven by the primal need to fulfill its own unique Destiny.

Historical pseudomorphosis can occur whenever a culture falls under the influence of a stronger one. For instance, Peter the Great of Russia made vigorous efforts at Westernization and succeeded in imposing the false form of Baroque Europe onto the emerging Russian culture. But it was a somewhat transient phenomenon, and Russian culture could well have recovered fully if it had foregone the Stalinist experiment. And perhaps it still will. Besides, Russian culture was and is very well separated from the Faustian—by history and geography and language—and so the false Faustian form could not be imposed directly enough to distort the Russian enterprise.

More to the point for our purpose here is the growth of the Magian culture out of the bowels of Classical civilization. Here the appearance was that nothing new had arrived. The primary language of the Magian emergence was Greek. The first Magian capital was Constantinople, founded on the site of the Greek city of Byzantium, first settled in the 7th century b.c.e. And the citizens of the Byzantine Empire didn't see themselves as Byzantines at all, but as Romans. To them the Roman Empire had been set up by the Lord God, Creator of the Universe, as a vehicle to establish and disseminate Christianity on earth, and though the capital had moved from Rome to Constantinople, the work continued without interruption.

So the Magian infiltration was stealthy indeed. Spengler cites the emperor Caracalla's granting of Roman citizenship to all free men in the empire (212 c.e.) as the first overt political indication of this change, since by this decree he erased the Classical custom of citizenship in the polis of one's birth, replacing it with an obligation to the greater State. But symbolic indications of Magian influence may be found in Rome a century earlier. As you may recall, I noted that for Spengler the architectural reification of the Magian space was the dome, and the first grand-scale dome in history was Hadrian's Pantheon, completed in 124. In fact, Spengler refers to it as the first mosque. The interior space of the building is vast and well-lit, perfect for accommodating a crowd. This is completely unlike the typical Classical pagan shrine, where the tiny dark cella held the statue of the god for the priest alone, with all the elegance on the outside, where the sacrifices were performed for the worshippers.

Of course as the name implies, the Pantheon was a temple to all the Olympian deities, quite a step away from the traditional Classical custom of local cults to particular gods, with each polis having its own divine patron (Athena for Athens, Apollo for Delphi). With the later Empire this universalizing spirit became the norm, with the old gods neglected in favor of new cults whose members believed that their deities encompassed All Things. Yahweh, Jesus, Helios, Attis and the Phrygian Cybele, Isis, Mithras, Ahura Mazda—each had a cult that held the god up as the source of all that is living and good.

Even so, the infiltration of Classical political structures with Magian social values was a gradual one. One institution that had to be established from scratch was the exclusive, intolerant community of belief. This was totally alien to the Classical state of mind, as shown by those early Magian cults centered on deities originally pagan. The believers who worshipped Isis, Helios, Attis and so on, though they claimed their deities dominated the big picture, still permitted the other pagan deities to serve in their myths as lesser characters, and they didn't concern themselves with rival cults at all. But once the exclusively Magian religions gained supremacy, such open-mindedness was swiftly outlawed. Following the Jewish model, the Zoroastrians, Christians and followers of Allah held toleration to be at worst a sin tending to bring divine retribution down onto the body politic, at best a courtesy extended to communities with whom one shared doctrinal origins. Thus the Byzantine Empire practiced a Christianity so bigoted that two of its internal controversies seriously weakened the State in the face of foreign armies: the Monophysites vs. the Orthodox (428–642) and the Iconoclasts vs. the Iconophiles (730–876). Islam, on the other hand, gave the "people of the Book"—Jews and the several varieties of Christian—freedom to operate their communities as they saw fit, so long as the political preeminence of Caliph or Sultan was acknowledged. Each community of believers was permitted to exploit the dogma space of its own choosing. Islam ran State policy, but it had the wisdom to let its more intolerant subjects each tag along in their own way.

Of course our purpose here does not involve intolerance, even in the context of historical morphology. Rather, we are concerned with the ways pseudomorphosis can be worked well, and ways it is done badly. We need to know what the Magian pioneers did that prospered them, and the things they did that brought bloody slaughter down upon them.

Much as it pains me to say it, in the context of imperial civilization, revolution does not work. Revolution is obviously effective during the contest between aristocracy and bourgeoisie that occurs during the maturation of a culture, but once the imperium has settled in, popular uprisings have no further prospects. Until its decrepitude is well advanced, the Imperial State that reigns over any civilization will easily annihilate any internal opposition so coherent that it can be targeted for destruction. The prime instances from the Classical are the Jewish Wars, with Triumphs to Titus and Hadrian. The Jews were crushed, twice. And this was in spite of the fact that the Jews had a complete and genuine rapport with the emerging Magian current, Jewish culture being the prototypical self-contained community of belief working out its Destiny within a coherent dogma space defined and even mystically embodied in a sacred text. But the political circumstances demanded pseudomorphic infiltration instead of violent self-assertion. Thus all the power they had accessed through their rapport with the Zeitgeist could only reify in the attainment of heroic immortality through military suicide. It worked well enough, I suppose, since the story of, say, Rabbi Akiba's last words (the Shema Israel, while being flayed alive) would help generate the self-identity the community needed to resist dissolution during the centuries of dispersion that followed. But mightn't a less assertive policy at the beginning have spared them the need for such desperate expediencies, simply by avoiding any dispersion at all? As it turned out, heroic martyrdom was the best they could make out of a bad beginning—perhaps ultimately successful in salvaging the situation, but nothing I have any desire to emulate.

More relevant to any program our sort might wish to encourage is the triumph of the Christian Church. Consumption by wild beasts in the arena notwithstanding, every aspect of the Christian strategy seems to have been intended to exploit the Classical infrastructure, using it as a vehicle for insinuating their Magian mind-set into every corner of the late Classical Mediterranean. The languages of the Church were Greek and Latin. Evangelism and Church business were facilitated by Roman roads, Roman shipping, and the civil order consequent to the Roman peace. Church administration was modeled on Roman civil government. And the propaganda of the early Church Fathers was designed for infiltration, this in the form of the "Apology," which came into fashion in the 2nd century. The works of Justin, Tertullian, Clement and Lactantius all sought to persuade educated pagans that Christianity was the culmination of their philosophical search, or the spiritual reflection of civil law.

It was only after political supremacy had been secured in the late 4th century that the Church was able to use civil law to compel the broader public to accept its dogma space as the only legitimate reality. And it was the previous three and a half centuries of quiet infiltration that enabled them to secure that supremacy, allowing for a working out of Magian Destiny without undue hindrance by either Classical reaction or barbarians from over the horizon, though the wheel, the rack and the arena were always there for those who chose the path of martyrdom. Of course Christianity became legal by the edict of Constantine, who also founded the

Magian capital of Constantinople, and it is at this point that the Magian character of the culture becomes undeniable. This supports Danilevsky's assertion that political independence is required for free cultural development. That anything we psychic technicians come up with will ultimately face this same need is made clear by the State's ongoing "War" against the Sacraments of the Snake, for the State will only abandon its aggression when it becomes something very different from what it is now.

But, again, such a transformation will have to be the consequence of a metamorphosis of the ruling class, not any sort of rebellion, since any violent effort at separation from a still-vigorous civilization sets the focus for that effort's own destruction. And non-violent efforts are always open to compromise. As we can see in the current political arena, objections to details in the operation of the status quo and efforts to correct them are indeed tolerated by the civilization, but only if these efforts can be assimilated by it. Thus we have the proliferation of advocacy groups, lobbying efforts, protests, petitions, and all the other attempts to effect "change through the System." Ultimately the movements with staying power will be accepted into the System as necessary corrections to the extremes inevitable in any market economy—whether social, environmental or whatever. But they will only be accepted on the System's terms, and if this is not possible they will be marginalized or destroyed.

One way the System recognizes causes that it may safely absorb is by the willingness, even the eagerness of their advocates to be *mediated*, to have their principles, personalities, proposals, etc. reduced to the text that occupies the space between the ads. A readiness to be **on television** assures the Powers That Be that the people involved are willing to be assimilated into the status quo. Which is to say, so long as their cause's issues are addressed, they will have no objection to themselves being made wholly Intellect in the best civilized manner. Thus they make themselves available to the various media, which drain their Blood like vampires to sustain the glamour of "living reality" that disguises the void that is their product. To participate in it is to be made a gargoyle in their façade—fixed in the minds of millions, made static in the image of their caricature, all virtue drained to vivify the illusion of Truth and Life that draws us into it.

Once any movement or cause has thus been made Bloodless, it may be incorporated or not within the status quo as makes no difference. But those enterprises that insist on maintaining a connection to Blood, and most particularly those that insist on developing innovative accesses to it, are ruthlessly suppressed. If, that is, they are foolish enough to call attention to themselves. The highest pitch of power, the greatest engorgement of Blood is permissible so long as no one else knows about it. Neither the World Corporate Order nor any civil government can audit an individual's store of power, or break that person's frame of mind. This is all the more so since they are blind to power and have no idea that there is a space *behind* the three dimensions they dominate, a realm of psyche available to anyone with the courage to enter it. Thus while pseudomorphosis will always remain problematic, it would appear to be the only possible strategy for transformation—the only alternative to the ultimate disintegration of the Faustian edifice and the attendant destruction of an infrastructure the planet can scarcely afford to rebuild from scratch.

The crux, it would seem, is to adopt and adapt Faustian technology to the extent needed to create the new in the midst of the old, but without succumbing to the unstated Faustian demand that technology must be regarded as a way to exploit Faustian space alone, to the exclusion of spaces psychic and spiritual. Paul of Tarsus used the Roman peace, the Roman roads, the Greek language and his status as a Roman citizen to disseminate the Magian religion he invented, and psychic technicians of today can promote their work through Faustian technologies for transportation, communication, psychoactive drugs and genetic engineering. Paul first encountered interference from the Roman authorities because his public preaching caused riots in the streets. But the Internet provides an essentially private forum for public proselytizing. The State has the power to investigate its contents, to be sure, but when there are millions of web sites, chat rooms, news groups and so on, what is their motivation in this age of dirty bombs and bioterror? Silence is a necessary prelude to any entry into psychic space, and once we obtain some mastery of that space, we can direct any necessary violence from its aetherial heights, through media invisible to any physical technology, and so attack the very substance of what our enemies perceive themselves to be.

But then what is this *psychic* space that I now invoke? There clearly is such a thing. Messy and subjective as it is, no one would deny that each psyche makes its own and populates it with entities that act on it. And no one would deny that occasionally these overlap from one psyche to the next; and that the coincidence of two or more spaces can result in agreement, cooperation, and even rapport. But there seems to be no unity to it, even though it seems there must be, and the possibility of a high culture winning its Destiny through its mastery seems far-fetched—much as the mastery of Ocean must have seemed to the Greeks and Romans.

Of course whether this psychic space reifies as an historical Next Step or remains the idealization of an esoteric fringe depends on whether there exists a means for accessing its levers and engines and turning them to our account. Claims of such mastery are as old as humanity. Shamans have made the journey to this realm from the very beginning, and every religion has offered options for taking power from it, even if entry and free action within it were forbidden. And since late Roman times there has been a more or less continuous effort to address it directly, to penetrate the traditional realm of the gods and tap their power to promote one's own purposes.

All these preliminary probes are consistent with Spengler's view of how cultures come to birth. He argued that precultural currents—currents coalescing into prototypes, then disintegrating, but the *type* remaining as the preliminary model for the next attempt—can precede the full-blown appearance of a high culture by several centuries. For instance, though Spengler dates the birth of the Magian at the year One, the Jews had their community of belief and their Torah by the time of their return from Babylon (6th cent. b.c.e.), an exact precursor of the coming Magian form. So if there is fresh cultural Blood about to flow out of a space adjacent to the Faustians' three dimensions, yet somehow unacknowledged by Faustian consciousness, we could expect that its well-springs will have been open for some time now. Much in the same way, it would seem, as our own.

VI. Psychic Space

Oswald Spengler was of the opinion that each high culture bloomed as a unique flower, without reference to any other cultures that had bloomed before or were blooming around it still. This, I think, misses the coherence of the greater process—the incremental domination of each and every space that humans can dominate. The "increment," in this case, is the culture. Each culture addresses a space that has never been confronted before, but still one that is within its power to master. And each culture can stand upon spaces mastered before its birth as it works to organize the peculiar space that it must confront right now. But it can have no regard for the distant spaces hiding within the mists of the unknowable future. For instance, we may suppose that the Egyptians and Greeks were well aware of the infinities that lay at the ends of the six directions. They just couldn't hope to control a space that vast, and it is through the conquest of a space that a culture captures its Destiny. So they each retreated to focus on something smaller: the line from birth to death to rebirth for the Egyptians, the beauty and power of the immediately present for the Greeks. And in the same way the Faustians have always known of the realm of psyche and spirit that I propose we now address. They just chose not to see it, or else saw it but refused to apply any common sense to understanding its dynamics, preferring to hold it back with either scientific detachment or crosses held out in trembling hands. *"Things men were not meant to know."*

Yet now that the Faustian enterprise is winding down, this space of consciousness and the psychic energy that animates it is opening up as if it were the New Frontier. After all, what else is left? And what does the human species need more? The Faustian enterprise has the technics to exploit the very Solar System, even to push aside the comets should they threaten collision with earth, but the mechanics of our own personalities remain a mystery to us. We can control everything but our own behavior, and by that we are baffled. And when our behavior includes religious intolerance focused through political paradox and armed with nuclear weapons, our whole social organism is in jeopardy. It is critical that the crisis be addressed. Rather than hold to Spengler's doctrine of the absolute independence of each culture's development, I think we can find more profit in looking at each culture-to-come as the next step to take after the ones that came before, and each special space as a stone to step upon. And by this criterion, psychic space lies before us, ready to take our weight.

The most straightforward definition of psychic space that I can give is operational: psychic space is the realm of consciousness that manifests as objective reality to the extent that psychic energy is focused through it in accordance with its characteristic dynamics. Given that reality is the objective residue of a subjective process, psychic space is where that process takes place.

The highway is hard; the traffic can kill you. They are as objectively real as anything can be. But both asphalt and semi-truck are the product of the massive physical and intellectual effort of thousands of subjectivities just like you and me. And depending on how much effort we put into making and maintaining them, they persist as solid, real things, often long after the subjectivities that originally conjured them have perished. But the subjectivity of someone, or everyone, is required to keep any one thing, and especially the whole thing, inflated with meaning. Without meaning, all these hard, real things all around us become so much clutter, no different from the stones, and no one cares if weeds grow up within the rust and broken concrete. Meaning being a psychic phenomenon like will and psychic energy, it appears as a feature in psychic space, giving will and psychic energy focus and coherence. And through this focus and coherence they cause our eyes and hands to recognize and fabricate the worlds we require.

Facing psychic space, then, with physical space our servant, we scarcely have any choice at all. We can master its contents or be destroyed by them. What Destiny such mastery may bring must remain beyond our comprehension, even if it lies within the vision of those who dare claim it.

The use of psychic space is nothing new. It is part of being alive, just like dying, appreciating what's in front of you, or traveling to the horizon and then over it. But when each of these three aspects of life was addressed as Destiny by a high culture (Egyptian, Classical and Faustian, respectively), the human condition was permanently raised in status. Mastery of psychic space is just another notch to push up to. By the deliberate manipulation of the mechanisms of this space we may flush out its full potential, if only we are willing to pursue its power across whatever spiritual landscapes the chase might lead.

It is difficult to say precisely when the deliberate manipulation of psychic space began. The dream time of the shaman had much in common with it, and mythical spaces like those used by the Egyptians and Greeks certainly shared characteristics with the psychic one. The energy web of Taoist magick can seem precisely congruent with it, except that the Chinese system is sclerotic with tradition. The modern exploration of this new space, on the other hand, has scarcely begun.

So as much from the need to make a start as any firm conviction that this is the place to do it, I will point to the 2nd century appearance of Theurgy. Theurgy was late Classical neoplatonic/hermetic magick in the high style, and I would call it the first calculated entry into psychic space.

"Theurgy" means "god-work," and the word was introduced during the reign of Marcus Aurelius by Julian the Chaldean, who used it to refer to magick that could influence the behavior of the gods. When combined with the systems of the neoplatonist Iamblichus and the school of Hermes Trismegistus, it became a regularized approach to magickal working.

In essence Theurgy assumed that divine energy is ubiquitous and may be accessed anywhere, anytime, if only we are able to come into rapport with it. To assist in the attainment of this rapport, the Theurgists had at their disposal the whole pantheon of pagan deities, demideities, nymphs and satyrs, and had access to the sacred rocks and springs, shrines and temples scattered all around the Mediterranean world, each one mythically identified with one sort of power or another. To the Theurgists, the act of worshipping a particular entity provided one with an opportunity to attain rapport with it and enter into its special level of energy. And so did they begin a Western tradition of using deliberately—which is to say, *strategically*—invoked mental states as a means for spiritual advancement.

With the political triumph of the Christian Church, the frankly pagan aspects of Theurgy were forbidden, but it persisted in strains of neoplatonic Christian mysticism and also in the Hebrew Qabalah. These scattered threads were brought together in a sort of neo-pagan synthesis during the Italian Renaissance, this particularly centered on the translation into Latin of the *Corpus Hermeticum* in Florence in 1463. Out of this came the work of Ficino, Bruno, Cornelius Agrippa, Paracelsus, and John Dee. But then the Counterreformation clamped down hard in the Catholic countries, and made harsh war on the Protestant. Bruno was burned and the Rosicrucians were exiled and forced to feign "freemasonry" in order to survive. Ultimately all was sufficiently coarsened that the Scientific Revolution had an open field for its triumph of Faustian technics. Psychic space was shut up in favor of a complete dominion of the three dimensions of physicality.

This all changed in the last hundred years or so—say, since the founding of the Theosophical Society in 1875. That the surge in occult thinking that followed has been so full-bodied indicates a fundamental degeneration of the Faustian forms that had kept it stifled for so long. This degeneration is just the sort of process Spengler identified with the transition from a condition of culture to one of civilization. In the case of Theosophy, of course, that is just what it was, the British Imperial Umbrella of Tolerance permitting a pantheistic, pagan world-view to diffuse throughout the Anglo-American hegemony.

Such liberalization is typical of this transition stage. But its roots go deeper than the necessities of an enlightened colonial policy. It has its source in the dynamics of the transition to civilization, and its ramifications are critical to those who wish to cultivate their Destinies in new spaces as yet unrecognized. Cultures resist the intrusions of alien forms. The Theurgic resurgence of the Florentine Renaissance was a direct challenge to the second estate of Faustian culture. And in the 17th century, both the Catholic and the Protestant arms of this second estate were quite muscular, capable of rubbing away all traces of the Theurgic upstart, save for such artifacts as Freemasonry. But in the process (particularly the Thirty Years War part of the process), Faustian culture stepped boldly into its maturity. The struggle aged it. It put its religious exuberance behind it and began such adult works as the perfection of technics and fighting the wars that would determine final supremacy. And now with this work completed, their essential Destiny accomplished and surrounded by the fruits of their labors, the Faustians sink down into the senescence of civilization. The social forms have gone flabby, their traditional guardians too compromised to muster the focus necessary to resist the essentially alien forms that intrude all around them. Nor do these guardians perceive a need to do so, so long as these new forms do not interfere with the essential business of making money.

These are important considerations for any who seek to introduce new cultural forms. This whole period of early, vigorous civilization is one of extraordinary fertility for cultural innovations of all sorts, simply because it is against the economic interests of the civilization to enforce uniformity. It was during the first three centuries of the Roman Empire that the founding prophets of the Magian flourished: Jesus, Paul of Tarsus, Akiba ben Joseph, Plotinus, Hermes Trismegistus, Mani. In the State of Civilization all Destiny has been accomplished, so for the status quo to strive to preserve old discipline seems an unnecessary effort. There are no more horizons to conquer. The horizons are covered with condos, and the important thing is to be in on the equity.

But when the leadership is thus preoccupied, those people who care less about equity and more about alien spaces brimming with Blood can pursue them as they will, taking possession of horizons no human has yet crossed. The only alternatives are to retreat from this frontier to search for something less audacious, or else sink into an unreflective indulgence in the fruits of civilization. But the less audacious Destinies have all been done, and the fruits of civilization are showing the spots that warn that rot is imminent. Besides, the enduring fragments of cultures gone and Destinies thwarted—most especially the explosive mix of Faustian technics and Magian apocalyptics—beg for some method of mastering human passions, some psychic technology that the passionate can use to transform all that energy into something that is actually useful. Faustian technics has brought us to the point where the human lack of control threatens annihilation. If the step into psychic space thus seems a big one, it is not so far as the short plunge into oblivion.

To put psychic space into an occult framework, I would say it is the realm of what Eliphas Levi called the astral light, which is our mental interface with what I have been calling psychic energy. Mind being a complexity of this light, our individual projections into psychic space may be considered as adjacent to or somehow coincidental with the collective, "objective" psychic space as a whole. Or at least they serve as entry points to it, since the collective responds to energetic inputs from the individual. If reality is the objective residue of a subjective process, it is the result of a consensus of all the competing subjectivities who contribute to it, from the ruling elite to the rank and file, from cats and rats to insects, viruses, and the trees and oceans and rocks—all adding substance to the mix according to their powers and purposes. By addressing psychic space as a thing in its own right we may observe this process and also manipulate it. Thus a knowledge of the natural laws that regulate it and the ground whereupon the contest is carried out will surely help us influence the outcome of any given situation.

Clearly, then, psychic space is open to all consciousnesses, however stuporous. Of course most have only the most elemental or ingrained means for imposing form, effective enough within their niches, but empty of originality except during rare crises of speciation. Even human creativity is mostly subliminal, consensual, habitual, entirely involuntary because the individual looks upon his or her experience and the beliefs that organize it as a personal approximation of reality, instead of as a creative process that he or she may adjust or manipulate to the advantage of his or her purposes.

A willingness to regard one's own passions dispassionately is the mark of the magician. By treating his (or her) perceptions and emotions and all the mechanisms of thought as objective, the magician may begin to exploit them. At the outset of his career he must become aware of the habitual nature of most of his stream of consciousness, and realize that many of these habits are completely counterproductive. He must devise ways to divert the psychic energy that animates these negative attitudes, redirecting the energy into something useful. As he wastes less power in emotional indulgence, the delicate interface between the vital force in his physical anatomy and the psychic energy behind his mental representation of it will become apparent, and the optimization of their mutual interaction will promote physical health and the accumulation of even more power. Eventually he will have sufficient quantities that he will be able to split it off and send it out into the world, where it may discharge as events that he can exploit to further his will.

Of course the crux of all this is that the magician treats his (or her) mental contents—the substance of subjectivity—as objects to be manipulated, and psychic space as the location where these objects are located. And yet the appearance of each person's psychic realm will be unique, as will that person's perception of psychic space as a whole, and so will the person's subjectivity—the tendencies of his or her unique personality—be projected upon psychic space in its collective sense. So at the same time that the magician steps back to manipulate subjectivity as an object, the magician interacts with this object, and the mutual objectivity beyond it, through an interface that is entirely subjective.

This is a paradox that profoundly disturbs partisans of the scientific method, which is mostly just an indication that the scientific method is incompetent to address psychic space. Every individual's psychic circumstances, and the data they get out of them, are unique, and hence cannot be replicated, nor may psychic energy be calibrated or quantified. Also, what we are manipulating is the very tool we use to do the manipulations, which is part of our identities, so it is impossible to separate the experiment from the experimenter. Science just doesn't work here.

Instead of scientific certainty, a healthy skepticism and a willingness to take psyche as we find it prevails in magickal circles. Take, for instance, the subset of magick called sorcery. Sorcerers work on the assumption that each definable vector of psychic energy may be treated as a separate, self-aware spirit with which the sorcerer may enter into a personal relationship—binding it to his or her will and thus gaining the authority to manage that particular complex's interaction with him. Whether psychic energy actually operates in such a personalized manner, or such spirits are simply projections onto psychic energy that allow for control over it, makes no difference to the sorcerer. By taking "the spirit model" as a working assumption, he or she gains a valuable tool for managing psychic energy, a tool that has worked reliably since the days of tribal shamans. Of course it is a tool that cuts both ways. So long as the sorcerer moves energy in accordance with the spirit model, he or she is bound to its logic whether spirits exist in "reality" or not. The sorcerer can use magickal techniques to manipulate them, but if this is done badly, they can take over in an obsession.

We only assert that the energy of psyche is real. The symbolic glamour is merely a mechanism we fit around it so we may manipulate it. But having built that mechanism, we are bound to its design. If the design is faulty or our manipulations are incompetent, our injuries will be real even if the mechanism is not.

It is here that we come to the fundamental difference between magick and religion. Both use some sort of symbolic template to focus psychic energy into specific purposes. But the magician does not care whether the symbols are true, so long as they are effective. Though a ceremonial magician will deal with gods, angels and demons, it does not follow that they have any identity separate from what the operator gives to them. They are tools for calling up, specifying and focusing energy, and as substantial as the energy is, so will be the result. They did not create the universe or send their sons to die for us. They don't care what we do with our genitals. They seek neither to damn our souls to hell nor to purify us so we may enter into heaven. They are tools for manipulating psyche and causing its energy to act to fulfill our wills—nothing more.

The religionists, on the other hand, will look on their beliefs as a gift of knowledge from the Being who made the Universe. Not only do they regard these beliefs as True in the Absolute Sense, but they may be willing to kill those who disagree, or be killed by them rather than renounce these beliefs.

And yet when we compare their approaches to conjuring, both magician and religionist appear to be exploiting the same psychodynamics.

Take, for instance, the dynamic of repression. It is well known in psychiatry, where therapists of all schools agree that repressed fears and rages invariably actualize as negative events in the repressor's life, either plainly self-induced or apparently "coincidental." But both magicians and religionists use this dynamic in a positive sense.

Magicians can conjure using their trained wills to repress all thought of a wish, except when they have energy available to charge a symbolic representation of it. They will generate the energy in ways ranging from ceremony to the dismemberment of unneeded beliefs to acceleration to sex and drugs and rock & roll. But when they are finished, they will allow themselves no thought of the symbol—until the wish is fulfilled or they have energy to charge the symbol again.

Religionists, on the other hand, having given over their lives to the deity, call their conjurations "prayers." Here also the desire is repressed. In the place of a will hardened with practices of yoga and asceticism, religionists apply the discipline of faith. Since they live for the deity and believe the deity has a plan for them, once they have expressed their needs through their prayers, their desires become the deity's problem, not theirs, and so there is no further need to think on them. And yet the desire will still exist *as need*, creating a certain tension. To the extent that this tension is kept out of consciousness *by perfect faith*, the energy can go into reifying the wish the prayer specified, in effect answering it. But if the tension caused by the juxtaposition of the desire and the lack of it suffers premature discharge in despair or spiritual pride, there will be no answer, just as a magician will be unsuccessful if he discharges the energy in second guessing or fantasies of success.

The dynamic that applies in all three cases—psychiatry, religion and magick—is that **energy will out**. If you do not express it by normal means, it will spontaneously erupt as a paranormal, miraculous or at least "coincidental" event, and always one consistent with the nature of the energy repressed. And so we have a tool for the manipulation of psychic space. There are many more.

While we are on the subject of magick, religion and belief, it would be appropriate to mention what Spengler offered as another symptom of the end of culture and the entry into the decrepitude of civilization: what he called "the Second Religiousness." This is the precise opposite of the magickally agnostic view just given. It also differs from the enlightened liberal orthodoxy that appears in the late stages of a culture, which perhaps will recognize a single spiritual summit, but will admit to many different paths to the top. Rather, the Second Religiousness is a return to the religious monomania of the culture's origins, a sort of spiritual second childhood. It will have recourse to the same dogmatic certainty, extreme practice and devout sincerity of its youth, but without the purpose of facilitating the Destiny of the culture, the purpose that made the faith so splendid back when the Destiny was new. That Destiny having been accomplished, the Second Religiousness will offer instead a place to hide from the moral disintegration attendant to this exhaustion of purpose. This does not mean that the magickal practice intrinsic to the religion will become in any way less effective, simply that what once inspired the culture's drive forward will now serve as a refuge from chaos. The same religious forms recur, ostensibly as an attempt to return to pristine beginnings, but working to insulate the believers from the horrors of the decline instead of giving them strength to accomplish a cultural quest. The quest is over, the civilization inevitable, and no faith can provide sufficient refuge from its decay. Our only alternative is to take from it what nourishment we can, sprout out of it like a fresh green shoot, and bloom as a flower never before seen on the face of the earth.

VII. A Model from Thermodynamics

To use the terms of thermodynamics, cultures are dissipative systems. Whether tribal culture or high culture, the human system takes energy from the environment and uses it—dissipates it—to produce the organization and artifacts characteristic of culture, and this out of a chaos of individual family units with no intrinsic need to cooperate. This is no great insight, but we might find it a useful one, for if we apply the principles of thermodynamics to cultures, we might discover why they go through their typical evolutions, and also find ways to bring new ones to birth once the old have become civilizations ripe for looting.

Energy is actual only in the act of its dissipation. Gasoline in a can just sits there, but when you pour it on the ground and set a match to it, it explodes as a storm of light and heat, the light rushing away in an instant, the heat pushing out on itself and into adjacent matter as quickly as its environs allow. That we have manufactured gasoline engines to force this heat to move us down the road simply means these environs can be contrived so the dissipation works to our advantage. But the dissipation itself is thermodynamic inevitability. The tendency is always toward energetic equilibrium, to any one part of space being in the same energetic state as every other. This is heat death, the cessation of all movement, the End. We are billions of years from this End but we still must rush towards it as quickly as we can, and the impetus to attain it is what animates the universe.

Once energy dissipates, it can never be re-concentrated without putting more energy back into the system. This is the second law of thermodynamics and the quantity that increases as energy dissipates is called "entropy." And when any system, from a clock to a star to the universe itself, has dissipated all its energy and stopped, it may be said to have reached a state of entropy.

The state of entropy is called the "attractor" for any dissipative system. A system's attractor is the state it tends to settle into. The attractor for a freely swinging pendulum is the point directly beneath it. The attractor for a river is the sea. These are known as "fixed point attractors," and entropy is surely a fixed point. But the concept of the attractor also applies to systems that defy entropy by receiving a steady supply of energy from the outside, though here the shapes become more complex. If you use an electromagnet to boost the pendulum so it doesn't stop, or if the sun evaporates the ocean so the rain keeps the river full, then the attractor becomes a circle. Attractors can be specified for systems made up of many interacting pendulums, for predator-prey systems, even for completely unpredictable systems like the weather. As the complexity of the system increases, so does that of the attractor, but what the attractor shows in all cases is the form of the interface through which energy can most easily dissipate itself.

All energy rushes toward entropy. It gets there as quickly as it can, unless inhibited by messy matter. If it gets caught up in matter it has to get out, and it will organize matter into quite striking arrangements if in this way it can get out more quickly.

Consider the energy of the sun. Spawned in the nuclear furnace at its core, it struggles for years to get to the surface, then flies outward at the speed of light. Most of it then dissipates without interference, but a tiny fraction strikes our planet and is trapped in its atmosphere. This energy, too, wants to plunge after its fellows into the oblivion of deep space, and much of it does so through simple radiation. But during the summer so much builds up in the oceans that radiation isn't sufficient. Instead it begins to organize water vapor into storms, then release the energy by condensing the vapor into rain. And not only storms, but swirling spirals of exquisite order that dissipate enormous amounts of energy—hurricanes—whose centers at their peak of power can appear to be perfect circles. The more energy the storm has, the more symmetrical its organization, as if its rush to dissipate the energy pushes the atmosphere into the shape that does that most efficiently. But when the storm moves over cooler water, or land, or the summer cools to autumn, the climate need not dissipate so much power and the organization collapses.

Compare this self-organization with our ability to contrive organization that will take advantage of energy's inexorable flow. If we can create a mechanism whereby the energy dissipates most easily by doing work for us, we will be causing the greater flow toward entropy to reverse entropy in the smaller sphere of our own convenience. In a gasoline engine the energy pushes out from explosive heat to the cool open air, and since the quickest way out is by making the pistons move up and down, it impels our vehicles down the road. A mill dam holds back the river's gravitational acceleration toward the sea and the mill race focuses that force so it will turn a water wheel on its way down, grinding corn or cutting wood. My body metabolizes sugars and oxygen to degrade them into carbon dioxide and water, and obliges the energy released to dissipate as consciousness, will and life.

The capturing of energy and using it to reverse entropy is a characteristic feature of living systems, from individual plants and animals to ecosystems and cultures. A rock will always roll down the mountain. Only an eagle will fly to the summit, or a human climb it, or a lichen spread up to the topmost boulder.

Living systems reverse entropy, but they are also dissipative systems. They reverse a quantity of entropy by dissipating a greater quantity of chemical energy. But obviously there is more to this than chemistry and physics. There is conscious purpose directing the anatomies that these metabolic systems animate, purpose whose fulfillment more or less advances the organisms' positions in their environments, giving them advantages they wouldn't otherwise have. The mechanism for the execution of this purpose may be genetic or instinctive, a matter of appetite or desire, the result of rational planning, intuitive understanding, the pursuit of Destiny or the Will of God. But one way or another living systems advance themselves in ways that defy randomness, producing contrivance in a world where, according to strict materialism, there should be none.

With this admixture of purpose we leave the strictly physical and enter the realm of the psychic, but that does not mean we are in any way liberated from our thermodynamic model. Living awarenesses may be regarded as dissipative systems in large part separate from the chemical systems that animate their fleshy bodies. They dissipate psychic energy as well as physical—the energy of consciousness directed toward the pursuit of purpose. The purpose pursued could range from the satisfaction of hunger to the search for a sex partner, from doing the spring planting to the discovery of the meaning of existence, but there will always be a direction for every awareness, more or less, a striving toward some goal. And the stronger the purpose, the greater the order spawned through the impulse to attain it. Just as physical energy rushes toward *entropy*, spawning physical order in its push to get there more quickly, so does psychic energy rush toward *satiety*, the accomplishment of the purpose, and it creates whatever sort of complexity that it requires in order to get there more quickly.

Whenever a physical system reaches entropy, it stops. And whenever a psychic system attains satiety, it lies down and rests. When water attains its level, the wheel stops turning. When desire has been fulfilled, the maintenance of a coherent effort seems too much trouble, and so the order that the effort called forth falls in upon itself.

And thus we get back to Spengler.

Just as physical dissipative systems exist on a multitude of levels, from quantum to chemical and biochemical to those of fluids like air and fire and water, so do psychic systems. From the lichen spreading to the top of the mountain to the Crusaders conquering Jerusalem, life devotes psychic energy to fulfilling some sort of purpose. And on the grandest scale, this takes place on the level of culture. As Spengler has it, the goal—the Destiny—of any high culture is the domination of the space within which its characteristic purposes are accomplished. And once this Destiny has been fulfilled, satiety sets in. The culture loses its momentum and all the vital forms it contrived in order to accomplish this Destiny stagnate into the senescence of civilization.

So we have similar dynamics working on the planes of physical energy and psychic energy, though none of this is so simple as two analogous realms moving parallel without interaction. There is necessarily interaction, because psychic energy depends on a continued flow-through of physical energy, and a large part of the psychic effort of any organism will be devoted to ensuring an ongoing supply of physical energy in appropriate forms. On the other hand, psyche can purposefully configure the material world so it is more productive of appropriate physical energy than it is in a natural state, as happened when we began to use agriculture to augment the supply of food energy. In one way or another, this extra energy will be disposed of. There can be an increase in population; the extra food can rot in the fields or in flimsy granaries; or other tribes who would rather go raiding than dig dirt can steal it. Or there can be a specialization of tasks, some people making sound granaries where food will keep, others becoming brewers, or metal workers, or soldiers to defend the new wealth, others administrators to efficiently allocate effort and resources. But such an organization will in and of itself require a vast infusion of psychic energy—both to organize and maintain it and also to induce the mass of tribal humans to abandon their autonomy in order to unite with the larger political body.

In Spengler's view, the disintegrating forces of personal and clan interest must be overridden by a greater purpose if people are to transcend tribal culture to enter high culture. This greater purpose is the Destiny of the culture, attained through the conquest of the space within which that Destiny is defined.

In terms of dissipative systems, Destiny is the *attractor* for the high culture. It is an ideal state that the culture's dominant estates can aspire to, a focus for their desire that will create a coherent flow of psychic energy whose push toward satiety will cause the culture to organize itself out of available ethnographic material. Such a Destiny might be recognized in the space between life and death, in the mastery of the immediately present, in the creation of a community in rapport with the will of the One True God, or in the domination of all things by controlling their physical circumstances. It is the higher purpose that inspires the elite to transcend clan identity to focus on the deeper problem. And so can the extra energy provided by agriculture create exquisite organization rather than degenerating into the burbling bloody chaos that ultimately makes agriculture impossible.

But then the quest to attain Destiny is a desire like any other. In Spengler's scheme, one thousand years is about how long it takes for a high culture's Destiny to be accomplished. And when it has been fulfilled, satiety sets in, which is the psychic equivalent of entropy, the end of the flow of psychic energy that kept the organization inflated and functioning.

With the accomplishment of Destiny the only life imperatives remaining are those that drive us in the tribal state: survival for self and clan. But of course the civilized economy is different from that of the hunter-gatherer. The hunter-gatherer has only the forest or the steppe to live from, while the citizen of a civilization has all the tools of the old culture at his or her disposal. So long as they can be kept running, the flow of physical energy will go on as before. If the feeling for the quest is gone, the economic apparatus has its own momentum, and gives rewards proportionate to the effort expended on it. It has energy to power it so long as the sun shines, if only it can maintain its coherence. But the flow-through of psychic energy that vivified the original culture will have stopped, and so does any impetus for renewal as well. The flow of Blood has dried up, satiety has been attained, and so one wonders just what overarching motivation there will be to maintain that coherence. The physical apparatus still chugs right along, driven by the need of each individual to *make money*, but can such a complex contraption long endure if each operator is only concerned with his or her own comfort? Spengler says no. Without the coherence that the push towards Destiny provides, the civilized populace becomes either fat prey for foreign predators or else turns on itself in corrupt self-absorption, no matter how finely the chains of law be forged.

In the language of thermodynamics, the culture will have reached a "bifurcation point," a situation where a dynamic system can no longer continue by building on its current status and so must either jump to a new level of organization or collapse in disorder. The old system no longer provides sufficient organization to dissipate energy coherently, so the energy either turns against the old order, amplifying its disorganization until it induces collapse, or else it is gobbled up by some new coherence that uses it to develop its own organization, one that is capable of supplanting the old order entirely. This new idea will be alien to the old order, but not necessarily foreign, perhaps a notion woven into the old culture's ethnographic origins but incompatible with its special approach to space and so disallowed from the accepted conception of reality.

Obviously of these two alternatives—collapse or the breakthrough into a new state—the second is superior to the first, though it won't be perceived as such by those who have identified with the status quo. They will see their established practice as the only one possible, essentially immortal if only it can resist the incursions of alien behavior, including of course the new cultural coherence that bids to replace it. Thus must there be a struggle between the new coherence and the status quo, which boils down to the stark choice between a blind quest into the unknown or a long, painful and entirely predictable dissolution.

And so we have a thermodynamic analogue for Spengler's historical dynamic of pseudomorphosis, and also a reason for his distaste for that dynamic and his own failure as a German political seer. That is, Spengler was enamored of the Faustian enterprise, had no willingness to search out or embrace any new thing, and only hoped that Germany could be inspired to pull itself together to win the rule over the Faustian decline. Being a man of that decline, he was not about to set out on any blind quests after unknown Destinies. There was still important Faustian business to be taken care of, meaning victory in the Wars between Contending States.

He was two generations too early to be worried about any Next Things.

Keeping to our thermodynamic model, it follows that this sort of bifurcation point will occur only when the culture is waning. When it is healthy, its Destiny will be pulling all available energy into the struggle to conquer its special space, and any who are involved in any separate quests will be conspicuously alien, starved for sustenance, and easily suppressed. But when this space has been mastered, psychic equilibrium sets in and all the energy previously devoted to the struggle will be available for anything. For the guardians of the status quo this will be wealth, power and brave self-indulgence. As such they will provide little effective opposition against those who share a vision of a new space, and feel the throb of Blood that must drive them into it.

With this "thermodynamic" model to assist us, then, we have the cold-hearted tool we need to apply Spengler's model without bias. A sense of Destiny is the attractor that draws the psychic energy that *knows* it must fulfill it. In its flow towards it, it creates the coherence of culture and all its apparatus and artifacts. And when Destiny is fulfilled, satiety sets in—psychic entropy, cultural death. The sun still shines and hence the economic apparatus continues to operate, but its future is over. For the present, the decay has hardly begun, but we may be certain it has long to continue. The true stasis of civilization is still some distance away, and getting there will be no fun. The dominant trend will be the imposition of an expanding corporate order as a defense against the Chaos infiltrating—both from within and without—through the disintegration of the old coherence. This corporate order will be a metastasis of Intellect, webs of policy and law strangling the last vestiges of organic culture, and against it no Blood can flow. The Faustian enterprise will grow ever more brittle, vulnerable to any sharp blow, and so will the Powers That Be grow ever more jealous of their safety. The Terminal State will establish its eternal rule, and if no new thing has grown up ready to replace it, *this* is where humanity's long fall from earthly preeminence begins.

VIII. What Comes Next

The Faustian Destiny was to conquer the three dimensions of space with its technics. This Destiny has largely been accomplished. Matter can be manipulated on scales ranging from atomic nuclei to asteroids; the genetics of plants and animals are available for our machinations; whole libraries of information can be stored on a single plastic disc[5]. Communication technology has reached a new apotheosis, the earth wired with a web of connections that threatens to turn we individual humans into mere neurons in its planet-girdling brain. The world has become one market in goods, services and ideas, with Pax Americana as its policeman, and those who would decry the pain inflicted by this "globalization" would do better to realize that they complain about the inevitable. Globalization was inevitable because the only thing that ever prevented it was distance, and Faustian technics have trivialized distance. All that remains is the iron law of supply and demand, and all the worlds billions in the same labor pool, available to the World Corporate Order as its needs demand. With the advantages of location and language now essentially eliminated, all are expected to compete on the basis of their talent and their willingness to conform to their corporate roles—to the extent there is any advantage in anything in this day of calculating machines, managing machines and hyperproductivity. While the struggle with matter still continued, the flow from desire to satiety was complicated indeed, complications that called forth the myriad forms that provided the culture with all its richness and complexity. Now our technics have eliminated all resistance—whether to production, distribution or consumption—and so those who had worked to eliminate those resistances and maintain those forms have become redundant. To even try to become one of the blessed few who work on the cutting-edge of technics seems like a gamble worse than a 7,000,000 to one

---

[5] If any would object here that much work remains to be done, I would concur. But I would also add that the fact that the effort of research has been institutionalized means that as a Destiny, it is done. It is no more a quest, but a matter of habit and profit, and there is no more glory in it.

lotto drawing. The lotto ticket only costs a dollar. An engineering degree costs $200,000 and four years of your life, and by the time you graduate you may be competing against someone in India or China who would be delighted to take as salary what a lazy plumber in America would disdain.

The last thing we should expect is for any member of the World Corporate Order to really care about this degeneration of the Faustian West, and this, too, is a consequence of the triumph of technics. Technics liberates Capital from locality. Where once Capital had to involve itself in politics just to protect its investment, and was loathe to risk itself in locations where the politics were unreliable or inaccessible, now every polity seeks to meet the standards of the World Corporate Order, so thoroughly dependent upon its cash have they become. Capital has become nomadic, its holders faceless, united only by their search for the greatest return. By its liberation from space, Capital has freed itself from all vestiges of the social contract. Having triumphed over the first estate and the second, the third estate now severs its ties to the fourth, the better to quest unencumbered after pure, abstract profit. It is not a situation that can be sustained, and Spengler sees three vectors for decay: Caesarism, depopulation and megalopolis.

Caesarism is a direct consequence of the death of a culture, the political reaction to the entry into a condition of civilization. With Destiny accomplished, the Powers That Be become too engrossed in making money, and too compromised by their efforts to do so, for them to govern effectively. Crises occur and so there are calls for a Caesar, a strongman who will resolve contradictions the traditional political forms are no longer capable of addressing. Once this decisive leader solves the problems, he or she will refuse to hand power back and will instead use it to personally resolve the intractable difficulties of the day. With this extra-constitutional authority, he or she sweeps aside the moneyed objections of the special interests and imposes order according to his or her own grand vision of the public good.

Spengler's Caesars are indeed "men-on-horseback," but absolutist reformers like Augustus Caesar rather than conquering heroes like Alexander or Napoleon. Caesarism can be an effective remedy for the political stagnation of an entrenched power elite so long as worthy Caesars hand their power on to worthy successors, a sequence that Rome could continue for only a few centuries. When it finally, inevitably breaks, the old forms of government will be so atrophied that they will lack the strength to impose succession, and in their absence the issue will be determined by civil war. Then all will be worse than before, and so begins the long descent into ruins, relics and ancient texts.

Caesarism must thus be seen as a political last resort, a radical cure beyond which nothing more can be done. The leader's personality and the bureaucracy he establishes are now required to do the work that the cultural forms once accomplished, which is acceptable so long as the leader is competent and alive. When this is not the case, there is only the force of arms to determine succession, until so many passes of the rake of war ensure there is nothing left to succeed to.

Historically, the reason Caesars gain power in the first place is a dire need for their military services. There will be an external threat, but the corrupt, self-interested government, incoherent with faction, will be incapable of dealing with it. Rather than going through the pain of correcting their own behavior, the power elite finds it more convenient to appoint the Caesar to call forth the unified response they are incapable of inspiring. For instance, the first Roman to whom Spengler gives the title "Caesar" was not Gaius Julius Caesar but Gaius Marius, called to the office of consul in 107 b.c.e. to deal with a stubborn war in Africa and an invasion of Cimbri and Teutoni from the north. Marius recruited an army from Rome's urban poor[6], trained it, and led it to victory, and so its loyalty was primarily to him. When the crisis was over he wouldn't give back his legions and kept power until it was torn from him.

As I write this (October 2004) the United States reigns as the world's sole superpower. The World Corporate Order works

---

[6] As opposed to the yeoman farmers of the past, who for the most part had ceased to exist.

unceasingly to impose commercial and hence political uniformity across the planet. Saddam Hussein sits in his cage and Osama bin Laden hides in the wilderness. It seems absurd to think that the situation could degenerate to the extent that such extraordinary authority would ever be given to a single individual. But then if Iraq splits three ways—even if done peacefully after the manner of Czechoslovakia—the consequent destabilization could result in a four-way war in the middle east. Since the United States Government is already operating under a staggering deficit, with an aging population heavily in debt, one wonders how well it could afford it if things got complicated. And if the nation is still as divided politically as it is now—with precisely half the electorate despising those who jammed the national foot into the bucket of tar that is Iraq, and half adoring them—resort to a Unifying Leader could seem like the only alternative.

But even if the situation with Islam and the middle east does not turn catastrophic, things need not get that bad next year, or even for the next few decades, for Spengler's model to hold. Spengler believed the Classical culture began around 1100 b.c.e., so Marius becoming consul would have occurred in its 993rd year. Since Spengler pegs the Faustian advent at 1050, that would make 2043 our date for the arrival of a civic savior. From the look of things, we're just a tad ahead of schedule.

Of course the turbulence that calls forth a Caesar could come from domestic discontent as well as a foreign crisis. Imagine that the World Corporate Order becomes so greedy, invasive and manipulative that it causes the "democracy" that it manages to spawn a secret state police force of unprecedented intrusiveness. By some quirk of Fate or morphological inevitability, an ambitious, insightful and capable person occupies an executive position in it. Recognizing the corrupt futility of the corporate agenda, this person gathers a cadre of kindred spirits from the officer corps of this force and together they seize control of it. Then for both love of humanity and his or her own glory, this person will grab the reigns of power to cause the State to take the people's lives back from the plutocrats. The people will reward their savior with absolute power for the rest of his or her life.

And of course when that's over, things get difficult again.

But Caesarism hasn't happened yet, and so now can only serve to remind us how bad it will get. Spengler's other two conditions, however—depopulation and megalopolis—are already hard upon us. As they continue to escalate, they make the chaos upon which Caesarism is contingent all the more likely.

Now when I refer to depopulation, I must emphasize I refer to depopulation within the Faustian sphere, not the world as a whole, a fact which may be a saving circumstance for the continuity of high culture on earth. Obviously the planet as a whole has far more people on it than it needs, or that nature in an uncontrived state could long sustain. But especially in Europe, and even in European populations in the United States, the birthrate has fallen precipitously.

I have a friend in Berlin whose profession is that of social worker. She already has two children, and so could be considered an impartial observer, and she reports a telling discussion amongst her younger colleagues during a professional conference a few years back. All of them were of childbearing age, yet none of them had children, and none of them had any plans for reproducing anytime soon. Unemployment was too high and their economic situations too uncertain for them to risk their middle class circumstances by having children. Of course also in Berlin there are thousands of Turks who think nothing of raising six or seven children without regard for life-style or even financial integrity. They are not Faustian, however, but rather fossil Magians, mere remnants until the great innovations of Faustian agriculture and public health exploded their population and sent them to Europe in search of employment. And something similar applies to the North Africans in France, the Hispanics and Asians in America, and the immigrants from across the Commonwealth in Britain—all non-Faustians with higher birthrates than the natives, demographic invasions more certain of success than any backed by force of arms[7].

According to Spengler, the depopulation of a culture is the inevitable consequence of the triumph of the third estate over the first. When the aristocracy is young its member's find their source of spiritual sustenance in the land. Their connection to it is a direct consequence of the need to hold it, by force of arms if necessary, and so they are tied to it by a bond of Blood. But once the third estate overcomes the first, the land becomes just another capital asset, the flow of Blood wholly channeled through Intellect. When rapport with the land is thus broken, one feels no compulsion to put back into it what one takes out—or at least it need only be renewed in terms of capital, that which may be expressed in the account books—Intellect, *not* Blood. Once this state of mind takes hold there is no longer any need to hold land in a family, and so family gradually becomes a non-issue. Not that there ceases to be satisfaction in children, but there is no more psychic necessity for them, and so one balances that pleasure against considerations of economics, appearance, comfort, career fulfillment, etc. Over the run of years, such considerations make depopulation inevitable.

This would be a good place to emphasize the inevitability of this progression of estates, and thus of the aging of the culture as a whole. The first estate, full of Blood and infused with a sense of *droit*, was quite capable of holding its land against Viking raiders, robber barons and greedy neighbors, but against bankers its efforts were futile. There could be no successful resistance to this evolution, because if the first estate in one nation does somehow keep the third in its place, they will be at a disadvantage against those neighboring nations where the commercial classes were triumphant. Two instances in Faustian history demonstrate the disadvan-

---

[7] For any who would call me racist here, let me emphasize that I'm neither objecting nor calling for resistance to any of this, merely pointing out how the present-day facts may be made to fit with Spengler's model. In America, even a complete halt to immigration would not reverse this ethnic transformation, though something could be said for it as a way to avoid added stress on the natural environment.

tages of delaying this inevitable growth: Germany and Poland. In both cases the minor nobility insisted on its rights and thus greatly delayed the formation of a national state. Germany was fortunate to have one state—Prussia—strong enough and ruthless enough to bring all its colleagues under its sway. Poland, on the other hand, ceased to exist for over a century, simply because a loose confederation of nobles, each fiercely jealous of his independence, is no match for the army of an integrated state, especially when the geography of the place is nothing but a steppe.

The triumph of Faustian technics has made the whole world such a steppe, with no resistance through distance to the exchange of goods, money, labor or destructive force. Those nations that resist the leveling tides of globalization can expect to be either overwhelmed or left high and dry. Not that globalization will necessarily be a better fate. Since technics have removed all impediments to economic equilibrium, the rush toward entropy will be incredibly swift, with only the plutocrats really benefiting. The great Faustian middle class will in time go the way of the dodo bird, most joining the urban mass, a few elevating themselves into the elite ranks of the commercially favored. And since the economic elite will have been globalized as thoroughly as the urban mass, one will hardly find Faustian characteristics here, either. As a culture the Faustian will have stopped, having attained its goal, and all that will be left is Anglo-American commercial custom and a habit of technics, the glues that keep the World Corporate Order intact.

Which leaves us with megalopolis, the most substantial—and already well-established—of Spengler's three monuments of civilization.

The defeat of the first estate meant alienation from the land; the victory of the third meant the attraction of the town. Towns became cities and of these a few were chosen by history and location to become planetary centers of wealth and power. Spengler saw megalopolis as a constant in every civilization, the demographic result of the money power's concentration in a few world cities: Rome, Alexandria, Antioch; Constantinople, Baghdad,

Cairo; London, Paris, New York. Where before there was conflict between the estates, and then between nations, now it is only between the cosmopolitans and the provincials, a struggle which the cosmopolitans always win—but at the cost of their connection to the land's beat of Blood.

> Long, long ago, the country bore the country town and nourished it with her best blood. Now the giant city sucks the country dry, insatiably and incessantly demanding and devouring fresh streams of men, until it wearies and dies in the midst of an almost uninhabitable waste of country. (II, p. 102)

Within the great stone city the connection to Blood is severed and one becomes wholly Intellect—beat replaced by tension, Destiny by Causality, custom by law. And as Spengler emphasizes, "Tension without cosmic pulsation to animate it is transition to nothingness. But Civilization is nothing but tension." (II, p. 103) Reproduction becomes an option, and then a bother, and finally a burden, but the city remains full because it has reduced the land to a means of production, causing the land's most ardent souls to leave it for the city's bright lights and infinite opportunities, it being the only place in civilization where ambition still pays. And when these are used up and the city finally falls in upon itself, the land will remain, inhabited by only the most stolid remnants, and so will the stage be set for centuries of ethnographic forgetfulness.

On the other hand, the overpopulation of the earth has made the supply of the ambitious practically endless, providing a steady supply of young replacements willing to enter the Faustian sphere to take up the tasks of the aging population. And Faustian technics has caused Spengler's web of Intellect to metastasize into every corner of the globe. There is no place anyplace that does not participate in the World Corporate Order, so even hermits on the mountain must compete as megalopolitans in order to survive. One merely needs to be wired in to receive the texts, and so can the texts define one's world, the flow of Blood all around becoming no part of one's concern, the land no sort of patrimony but just a place to stand while one's Intellect manipulates the data.

But this gives us cause for some hope, at least. With megalopolis everywhere, there is less compulsion toward that hopeless urban overcrowding and the devastating desertion of the countryside that is civilization's hallmark. On the other hand, when the whole world has been wired as if it were a single city, it becomes extraordinarily fertile to those dangerous ideas that are the seeds for cultures-to-come. Individuals can communicate instantaneously without regard for cost or distance; concepts can circle the globe in days. Paul of Tarsus infiltrated Magian culture into Roman civilization with Roman roads, the Roman Peace, and the Greek language. So we have the Internet, Pax Americana, and English. And more than Rome ever was, Faustian civilization is a creature of information. Its efficient physical functioning depends on an instantaneous exchange of information, and most of its wealth is contingent upon the continued existence of the information infrastructure. (Of what use is a media center without media, or a new Mercedes without an authorized service provider?) At the same time, information is generally transmitted as text. And text is dead. Squiggly lines on paper or the digitations of a DVD, we can only say that it exists—perhaps the only thing anywhere that does just exist, rather than having something it can actually do. *Only when a living intelligence enters rapport with a text can it have any effect at all,* meaning that the entire existence of the planet-spanning Faustian megalopolis and the web of control that maintains it *is dependent upon a state of mind.* There need be no plagues or urban chaos to accompany its inevitable end. Something entirely new could begin with the simple decision to toss away the pager and unplug the computer. Thus if people see the advantage of addressing space in a new way, and encounter a special sort of Destiny in that new space, one which lets them partake in a fresh flow of Blood, might not megalopolis then be emptied in a day?

And no one would even need to pack.

IX. Strategies

The process of cultural evolution must necessarily be different for cultures born alone out of ethnographic material and those that must emerge within the midst of a still-vigorous civilization. The Faustians, rising up from the forests of Western Europe a thousand years ago, had only the wilderness and each other to struggle with as they made their new beginning. The founders of Magian culture, on the other hand, lived in the midst of Rome at its mightiest, and many a martyr was torn asunder before Magian political supremacy brought personal safety. Our present circumstance clearly has more in common with the Magian emergence than with the Faustian. This is simply a fact we must make do with, for there is nothing to be done about it.

I mentioned one aspect of this "making do" in the section on pseudomorphosis—the need for non-confrontational infiltration—but there has to be more. There has to be something gleaming, pure and holy about the new culture that will inspire the best part of the civilized populace to shift its orientation from the Old space to the New. The culture that stands up alone out of the wilderness is the only game in town, so it doesn't need to win converts. But a culture emerging in the midst of a civilization has all the fleshpots of decadent materialism to compete with—whether bread and circuses or Wal-Mart and the World Wrestling Association. To attract a population large enough to endure, the culture that quests into the new space must offer something beyond the imagination of the civilized Powers That Be, filling a gap they are constitutionally incapable of recognizing.

The trait the Classical seemed to lack, especially among the Romans, was simple humanity. Roman culture was vicious. From the treatment of slaves to the disregard for the poor to the arena spectacles of gladiator fights and prisoners devoured alive by wild beasts, an acceptance of human suffering was ubiquitous. Against this the Christians put the proposition that man was made in the image of God, that God's son died to redeem the individual, and that charity to its less fortunate members was an obligation of the community. That this Magian innovation left the Classical leadership at a loss is shown by the reaction to it by the Emperor Julian, nephew of Constantine the Great and leader of the last pagan revival. In his "Fragment of a Letter to a Priest," he admonishes his recipient to take more care of the less fortunate in his city, because charity to the poor was "the impious Galileans'" prime tool for conversion. He goes on to compare the Christians who sponsor the *agape* feast to slave traders who throw food to children so the children will follow the traders until they're away from their families and the traders can safely kidnap them. "By this method, I say, the Galileans…have led very many into Atheism." (305c)

Which is not to say that Julian denied the callousness of the Roman establishment. He asks what good would come if the gods rained gold upon the poor, "for even though this should come to pass, we should forthwith set our slaves underneath to catch it, and put out vessels everywhere, and drive off all comers so that we alone might seize upon the gifts of the gods meant for all in common." (290 a–b) His whole letter is an admonition to his subordinate (as emperor he was *Pontifex Maximus*) to correct the deficiencies in pagan governance so that established religion could beat back the threat of the insidious Galileans. But Julian's reign was late enough that the Magian current was open and aggressive; his own cult of King Helios was itself one that Spengler identified as Magian. So Julian's empathy is less surprising than it would be coming from a Crassus or a Hadrian. His willingness to have paganism embrace the ethic of community welfare is entirely consistent with his time.

The question for us now must be: what is the Faustian blind spot, and what do we partisans of psychic space have that will fill it? I would submit that the gap for the Faustians is the way they privilege institutions over individuals. This they do through their readiness to grant corporations—contrivances of finance, text and law—the same rights as human beings, miraculous unions of spirit and flesh. That the corporation would be granted this privileged status is wholly consistent with the Faustian imperative, since any attempt to dominate the six directions of space must involve a group effort. The viability of the group is paramount, and though the heroism of individuals is celebrated, service to the organization rather than personal honor is the criterion for heroic action.

Now by "corporation," I refer to the incorporated entity in the strict legal sense, meaning most any institution involved in *anything*: commerce, religion, charity, environmental action, political action. All will be incorporated, from business to hospital to church, and from their special status in Faustian law, they gain the privilege of becoming "persons," yet at the same time have their obligations circumscribed in ways not possible for a private person. Between the ubiquity of the corporation and the rigidity of the State (which instead of "limited liability" has "sovereign immunity"), there isn't much left for the individual. And naturally corporate resources are in general vastly greater than those of individuals. The combination of legal standing and infinite resources leaves little doubt whether corporation or human individual will prevail in any open conflict over the long run.

On the level of personal life in the Faustian, this privileging of the corporation is shown by the practical immunity from retribution that individuals acquire when they act as the willing servants of corporations, their personal responsibility subsumed under the legal fiction of "limited liability" that protects the organizational persona. That people in general see such submission as the norm is made clear by the subtle suspicion a person encounters if he or she is not somehow affiliated with an incorporated entity. Much of this has an economic basis, since it is rather hard to live in Faustian circumstances unless one is employed by a corporation, any more than one could live in Magian circumstances without membership in a religious community, or in Classical without citizenship in a *polis*. So we shouldn't be surprised to see a deeper level of distrust as well. It is as if one must be suitable for membership in a larger concern to be worthy of people's confidence, or even their interest, so without some greater sanction one is on the fringe indeed. Of course such isolation may soon be economically impossible as well as socially awkward. As the corporate reach extends to all aspects of life, there will be ever fewer niches that an individualist can occupy.

The Faustian space has now been dominated, the Faustian Destiny fulfilled. But the corporate prerogative finds itself everywhere extended, nowhere abated, and every advance in technology augments their power to impose control. With work everywhere becoming more computerized, electronic availability ever more inescapable, and software now perfected that lets an employer record *every keystroke* an employee makes, even the preconscious eruptions that are the well-springs of the creative process become subject to correction according to the requirements of policy. To remain employed, one will have to acquiesce to being permanently "on-line," to submit to personal reengineering according to the standards of one's duties within the corporate mission. Hulking bodiless before the screen, hypnotized by dead text glowing phosphorescent, cut off from fire, water, air and earth, one is insinuated into a condition of pure Intellect, one's nervous system becoming an especially adaptable processor powered with a carefully calibrated supply of Blood, a reprogrammable bit of fleshware entirely at one with the planetary net that is the World Corporate Order.

Now one may ask, "What happened to the quest for individual glory that came with the birth of the Faustian enterprise—the cult of honor among the aristocracy, the thrill of single combat, a fast ship, and a sack full of loot?" I would answer that such assertive individuality was never really a Faustian virtue, being instead a strain of uncharacteristic ethnographic material that attached itself to the Faustian political enterprise in much the same way as Aristotle and Euclid attached themselves to the spiritual. And just as the second estate expended centuries of effort getting rid of Aristotle and Euclid, so the first estate has had to endure centuries of discipline to rid itself of the old chivalrous ethic, thus allowing for the creation of armies that could dominate all three dimensions of space and hold them for subsequent exploitation. And the corporate citizen is the soldier in the line of economic battle. There never was any room for glory, except in service to the corporate whole. The best one can hope for is to be *vested*.

The imposition of corporate uniformity is the essential brutality of the Faustian enterprise. Beyond the reach of this hypertrophied tool for the conquest of a space now dominated, I point out a new sort of space, psychic space, which is a magickal space. The features of this space consist of meaning and purpose animated by psychic energy. The entryway into this magickal space is entirely individual, and it is soaked in subjectivity. Thus it is something no corporate strategy can possibly encompass. They may attempt to manipulate aspects of this space (advertising is an obvious attempt), but they cannot address the space as such, because to do so they would have to become very different people than what they always thought they were. In this space, legal fictions like corporations and civil government can have no presence *except for what is given to them by the thoughts and habits of the self-aware beings who participate in them*: members and customers, vendors and victims. Thus the reality that an institution enjoys does have a representation in psychic space, but it will possess no duration there beyond what those living persons who are involved with it decide to grant it. Its cohesion can only be maintained by will—by the consent of the governed, as it were—but in this space it is a consent that may be withdrawn, or simply lapse through inattention. Thus the institution loses all its advantages here, the privileged status going instead to individual possessors of consciousness. They are the sole source of psychic energy available for building the power structure, and the only ones able to focus it to apply control.

 This is not to say that the culture of psychic space will not have its preferred mode of social organization. Just like the *polis* in the Classical, the community of belief in the Magian, and the corporation in the Faustian, there will be a characteristic way people work together to fulfill Destiny. Logically its members would want a way of facilitating collective, coherent psychic action, which might involve some future perfection of present-day covens and magickal orders and so on, or it could involve spontaneous coherences around specific purposes, facilitated by the Internet. But it will emphatically *not* resemble a present-day governmental or corporate organization. How cohesive such Faustian organizations manage to remain will depend on their members' rapport with the organization and with one another, a rapport that may to some extent be manipulated by magickal principles. It's hard to imagine an FBI or an Exxon-Mobil becoming a cult, but I expect they will try before their entire constituencies transform themselves into something that will not even admit to their existence.

In the meantime we can expect such Faustian entities to grow ever more arrogant in their civilized satiety, ever more conscious of their legal prerogatives. As they pursue these, they will strive to exploit what has up until now always been considered territory to be held in common. Vast reaches of these meta-Faustian spaces lay open, waiting for enclosure by the cyber-industrial revolution, with even the human genome being claimed as private property, fenced in by whatever legal barricades the World Corporate Order is able to erect and maintain.

The day I first wrote these passages (14 March 2000), the NASDAQ Stock Exchange Composite Index lost 4% of its value in a few hours, this on the news that President Clinton and Prime Minister Blair had reiterated the previously implied policy that the raw data of the human gene sequence must remain in the public domain. For so much value to vanish because of a mere reminder indicates what a vast surge of commercial will (i.e. greed) such State policy holds back. As the political forms grow ever more soggy with compromise, and the scientific boundaries ever harder to define, this dike will turn to an ooze that slowly covers all things human, and even our very biological evolution will become subject to the requirements of corporate cash flow. The whole tide of economic and technical progress favors this corporate invasion of all flesh, and the efforts of God-fearing conservatives will not stop it. As I write this revision (March 2004), South Korean breakthroughs in the fields of stems cells and therapeutic human cloning threaten to turn the Bible-bound USA into a biotech backwater, quite the opposite of the "leader through innovation" it is supposed to become in order to counter the outsourcing of jobs consequent to globalization. But this disadvantage should not last. In the end I have faith that money will push aside even the most neophobic Second Religiousness, and that the inexorable tide of technics will open a way into the centers of our very cells. Then may the apportionments of Intellect supplant all need for Blood so that Faustian civilization can be liberated from Spengler's grim round to become an immortal city that spans the planet, staffed by the optimum population of perfectly manufactured humans.

Opposed to this vision is that of those pioneers who would rather manufacture reality than be manufactured by it. Far beyond the realm of fabricated humanity there lies a space where reality itself stands open to manipulation, if only we be so bold that we can step into it. Of course by doing so we perforce abandon the reality we had depended upon up to that point, the one we had been taught from birth was the only one available. But it is beginning to seem so very tattered, with an uncertain future, and if there are alternatives that can be made to work...

X. "Form," Race and the Nazis

Spengler notes that a vigorous culture will have a strict "form" that its members will aspire to, and that to participate fully in the culture they must be "in form," which Spengler interprets as being "in training," just like an acrobat or a race horse. Only then can the person have the discipline, skill and wit to master the form and thus reach the intense pitch of achievement necessary to produce and maintain high culture.

As a general rule, such a form will create and maintain culture by providing the cohesion needed for a group effort within a given estate, be it aristocracy, priesthood or bourgeoisie. Because of the consensus the form imposes, the group's members will not only instantly understand one another, but will act in the synchronized manner made possible by their intimate awareness of what is expected of them. Born into the form, educated with the expectation that they would fill their positions as their parents had, the incapable would find themselves shuffled off to lesser things even as the *esprit* of the fit attracted candidates from the lower classes, the most capable of whom could earn admittance to that "band of brothers" who "make history" in the arts and technology, in priestcraft and in war

But then what happens when such a social order's physical territory has been infiltrated by those who do not participate in its form? An attenuation of cohesion, no doubt, even social discord and a weakening of the body politic.

It is with this idea of cohesion in mind that Spengler introduces the idea of *race*. To Spengler race had nothing to do with genetic heritage. Humanity is too muddled to pick any one 'ethnic identity' as the 'pure' stock. For Spengler racial identity was determined by generations of shared economic, political and geographical experience, with the ones who participated in it acquiring membership in that race, regardless of where their ancestors came from.

These were the parameters that framed Spengler's view of the "Jewish problem" in Europe. For Spengler the Jews were simply members of the Magian civilization placed by history in the midst of Faustian culture, but scarcely capable of joining in with its youthful enthusiasms. Since Magian social order was built around communities of shared religious belief instead of shared language and geography, it was possible for Jewish communities—separate entities within Europe's growing towns—to survive without contamination by the Faustian current. Since Magian religious consensuses are transnational, a Jew could enter any ghetto in Europe and feel essentially at home. And since all branches of the Magian were thoroughly into the stage of civilization by the time the Faustian culture began, the Jews—like the Greeks, Syrians and Lebanese—possessed a money-consciousness that was highly refined, just like the Americans and Europeans today. But so long as their primary contact was with the land, the Faustian money-consciousness was rudimentary. The Faustian current did not produce a banker of note until Cosimo (the Elder) de Medici, who flourished in the mid-15th century. But Faustian statecraft had required bankers from the beginning, and since the Greeks were in Greece and the Lebanese were in Lebanon, that left the Jews to take the consequent resentment on that score. At the same time, the dynastic struggles and the virulent regionalism that animated Faustian politics could have little meaning for any Magian soul. Spengler points out that in later centuries, those European Jews who chose to involve themselves with Faustian politics tended to do so with a transnational bias. In Eastern Europe, they were partisans of the Socialist International. In Britain, they were imperialists. Naturally, then, their behavior was always suspect in Faustian nativist circles, their alien religion and closed communities making conspiracies and collusions easy to imagine. And thus was the foundation for a virulent anti-Semitism laid down.

Spengler would have none of it. The solution for him was assimilation. As the Faustian culture entered the "historyless" stage of civilization, the "historyless" Magians within their midst would be able to reach an understanding with its members. Ultimately the fossil Magians would blend seamlessly with the fossil Faustians to make up the ethnographic material remaining when the decline of the West had reached bottom. This sort of assimilation was well in hand in Britain, France, Italy and the Low Countries in 1922, when Spengler published his analysis in the second volume of *The Decline of the West.*

Now if the disinterested interpreter is obliged to admit that Spengler's political thought contributed to the horror that began fifteen years later, it wasn't Spengler's interpretation of the race question that got him into trouble. In fact, that was what helped him keep his hands clean. His political program was more concerned with national discipline than such details as the religion of those who handled state debt. His vision was of a return to the old aristocratic forms of excellence, of a broad desire to be "in form" as a way of demonstrating self-worth. Only through this restoration of cultural discipline could Germany have the strength to triumph in the final phase of the Wars between Contending States. Once this period was over, the degeneration intrinsic to the civilized condition would infest Germany as much as every other part of the Faustian sphere, but if Germany were victorious, it would be the better for it. History would be over and the Reich would be the center of wealth and power, the best place to be during the long slide into ethnographic forgetfulness. So there had to be a return to the old forms, to the condition of being "in form," and for this Spengler reiterated his emphasis on assimilation. In his *Jahre der Entscheidung* ("Year of the Decision"), published in 1933 just as the Nazis were coming to power, Spengler noted that from the Franco-Prussian War onward, the German bourgeoisie began to push upward into the Prussian officer class, this in spite of their not being bred for it in any genealogical sense. And yet Spengler was all in favor of this. This was the way class was supposed to work. The best and the brightest of the class below would be admitted to the class above according to their ability to apply themselves to its form. Their presence in it would be somewhat artificial, to be sure. They wouldn't have the easy movements of one born to it. But their children would, and so would their ardent Blood go to animate the traditional practices of rulership that kept the nation "in form," creative of high culture and strong to resist the incursions of rival nations within the culture, and also those from the outside (e.g. the Soviet Union). And though Spengler does not explicitly say it, it seems reasonable to assume, at least theoretically, that a Jewish burgher could participate in the Prussian form as well as a Christian one, assuming he had abandoned the strictures of kosher living. It should merely be a matter of being willing to embrace it as a way of life.

Unfortunately for Germany, there were others who held to a debased version of this vision of excellence. The Nazis asserted with violence their belief that a person's ability to be "in form"—and hence to keep society "in form"—did not have to do with one's willingness to aspire to a standard of honor, physical and mental courage, and military discipline, but instead was a matter of dialect spoken, preference of food and drink, religion and ancestry. And in a psychotic attempt to make their debased vision real, they initiated a program of mass murder that may well have caused Germany to lose the war, simply through loss of skilled labor, loss of military manpower, diversion of military resources, and the policy's tendency to spawn fanatical partisan resistance.

The Nazis' version of Spengler's program was Spengler-made-stupid to appeal to all that was bigoted and resentful in a desperate electorate. Because Spengler was no democrat, because his appeal to the youth and his pro-industry economic thinking were so similar to the Nazis', and because his rhetoric implied that a belligerent foreign policy was justified, it was easy for an uncritical observer to see Spengler and the Nazis as essentially the same. In that case a German of the period could honestly say that he had been encouraged by Spengler's vision to swear allegiance to the Führer. And to that small extent Spengler does bear responsibility for what followed.

But none of this invalidates Spengler's system of historical morphology, only his inappropriate application of it. His attempt to rehabilitate the aristocratic forms that were his ideal was foredoomed to failure by the historical dynamics his morphology so well described. Faustian culture was stiffening into civilization, so the triumphant strategy would not involve disciplined conformity to an ancient form, but the ability to assemble an international coalition and supply it with the most vigorous industrial base. Spengler's belief otherwise was akin to one saying that Octavian defeated Antony because he called upon the yeoman virtues of the Roman peasantry—in that such virtues had been used up by the end of the Punic Wars. But Spengler's error here was merely a philosophical mistake. The tragedy was his attempt to promote his position like a man of practical politics, for it made him available for co-option by those who needed the aura of Truth that clung to him from his morphology. They produced a degenerate version to appeal to a less discerning public and to justify the necessity of their enormous crime.

Spengler, to his credit, was able to evade almost all personal participation in this perversion of his work, a feat made possible by the unshakable integrity of his intellect. As early as 1924, in his essay "Reconstruction of the German Reich," he had written that ethnic preferences were counterproductive when it came to practical politics. Many of Germany's rivals had done very well being ruled by ethnic outsiders: Catherine in Russia, Napoleon in France,

Disraeli in Britain. Also, many typically German traits were hardly conducive to national cohesion: internationalism, pacifism, and a foolish romanticism that tended toward anarchy. Spengler suggested that foreign ethnic stock was a boon to the nation because if such populations are given a chance to assimilate, they will enthusiastically embrace the land that adopted them.

There was one small private compromise on Spengler's part. In the election for Reichspresident in April of 1932, Spengler voted for Hitler instead of the conservative (though somewhat senile) Hindenburg, who won. It's hard to understand this lapse, given Spengler's aversion to the Nazis' coarseness and self-righteous ignorance. He once remarked to his sister that Hitler was "ein Dummkopf," but one had to support the Movement. Apparently he thought the Nazis offered the best chance for national unity, given the Bolshevik threat from the East and the eternal enmity of France in the West.

But three months later Spengler redeemed himself. Six days before the Reichstag elections of 31 July 1932, when the Nazis scored their greatest triumph, Spengler and Hitler met at the Wagnerfest in Bayreuth. The two men conversed for about half an hour, with Hitler doing most of the talking, though Spengler was able specifically to refute Hitler's position on race. When the encounter was over, it was evident to those present that their disdain was mutual. And when Goebbels twice tried to persuade Spengler to give his public support to their regime, Spengler's answer was two refusals. With the consolidation of Nazi power, Spengler became *persona non grata*, and the German press paid no more attention to his existence.

Before that happened, however, his publisher was able to issue the previously mentioned *Jahre der Entscheidung*. Apparently Spengler believed there was a chance power could still be wrested from the Nazis, for the book appears to be an attempt to be as belligerent and reactionary as they in all things economical and political, even as it eschews their bigotry, pageantry and casual brutality. Thus to modern ears the book at times reads like the ravings of a Neanderthal. It was as if Spengler was all in favor of the Coming Struggle, so long as Germany had a competent Caesar to lead it. The book appears to be an attempt to persuade the electorate to find someone who wasn't Hitler to lead them to the same place Hitler said he would take them, though without the political religion and the "racial purity."

Of course he failed. The contest he predicted and encouraged came to pass, but without any improvement in the leadership situation, and so was defeat made inevitable. And now the situation largely conforms to the scenario given in the *Decline*. Money rules. It rules every tycoon and tenant on the great asphalt web that covers the green land. But because *Jahre* was Spengler's last statement, it will always be there to represent an aspect of his thought that simply tastes bad, and leaves a sort of unsettled feeling in the pit of one's stomach. Though in its emotionalism and partisanship it is the antithesis of the farseeing perspective of the *Decline*, the *Decline* can't help but be shadowed by it.

Even so, time marches on and the relevance of Spengler's historical morphology grows ever more frightening, the ongoing strangulation of Blood by Intellect having become an aggressive, almost palpable process. Spengler was correct in his overall analysis, even if unfortunate in the fate of his homeland. And there is plenty of hope to be found in his morphology if only one examines its fundamental assumptions, as I have tried to do in this essay. They are there for us to apply, if only we have the wit and the will to do so. Spengler wrote his last just as the European boil was coming to a head, and so his final expression naturally seems somewhat inflamed. But that boil has burst and bled and drained and healed over at last, and the top man in the Kremlin can sound a lot like Danilevsky. Spengler largely concurs, but is more intuitive. We could do worse than to listen.

Bibliography

Austin, John L., *How to Do Things with Words*, Harvard, Cambridge, 1975

Campbell, Joseph, Primitive Mythology, Penguin, New York, 1976

Crowley, Aleister, *The Book of the Law*, Samuel Weiser, New York, 1976

   Eight Lectures on Yoga, Sangreal, Dallas, 1969

   Magick in Theory and Practice, Castle, New York, n.d.

   The Vision and the Voice, Sangreal, Dallas, 1972

Derrida, Jacques, "Plato's Pharmacy," *Dissemination* (trans. by Barbara Johnson), University of Chicago, 1981

Dudley, Donald R., *The Civilization of Rome*, Mentor, New York, 1960

Green, John Richard, *A Short History of the English People*, J. M. Dent, London, 1915

Hakim Bey: The works of Hakim Bey may be found on the World Wide Web. The works cited are:

   Chaos: The Broadsheets of Ontological Anarchism, 1985

   "Permanent TAZs," 1993

   Radio Sermonettes, 1992

   The Temporary Autonomous Zone, 1990

Hughes, H. Stuart, *Oswald Spengler: a Critical Estimate*, Charles Scribner's Sons, New York, 1952

Iamblichus, *On the Mysteries* (trans. By Thomas Taylor), Wizard's Bookshelf, San Diego, 1984

Flavius Claudius Julianus, *The Works of the Emperor Julian* (trans. by Wilmer Cave Wright), William Heinemann, London, and Macmillan, New York, 1913

Kirk, G.S.; Raven, J.E.; Schofield, M.; *The Presocratic Philosophers*; Cambridge University Press; Cambridge; 1983

Mouzelis, Nicos Panayiotou, "Bureaucracy," *Encyclopedia Britannica*, Chicago, 1979

Nicol, Donald M., "Byzantine Empire," *Encyclopaedia Britannica*, Chicago, 1979

Plato, *The Dialogues of Plato* (trans. by B. Jowett), Oxford, Humphrey Milford, 1924

Prigogine, Ilya, and Stengers, Isabelle, *Order out of Chaos*, Bantam, New York, 1984

Shirer, William L., *The Rise and Fall of the Third Reich*, Simon and Schuster, New York, 1960

Sorokin, Pitirim A., *Modern Historical and Social Philosophies*, Dover, New York 1960. (Sorokin is my primary source for Nikolai Danilevsky. There is no English translation of *Russia and Europe* except for the excerpts Sorokin translates himself.)

Spare, Austin Osman, *The Book of Pleasure*, 93 Publishing, Montreal, 1975

Spengler, Oswald, *The Decline of the West* (trans. by Charles Francis Atkinson), Knopf, New York, 1957

The Hour of Decision (English title for *Jahre der Entscheidung*, trans. by Charles Francis Atkinson), Knopf, New York, 1934

Swassjan, Karen, *Der Untergang eines Abendländers*, Raphael Heinrich, Berlin, 1998

Vaihinger, Hans, *The Philosophy of "As if"* (trans. by C. K. Ogden), Routledge & Kegan Paul, London, 1935

Xenophon; "The Memoirs of Socrates;" *The Works of Xenophon, Vol. IV*; J. Walker, F. Wingrave, R. Lea, et al.; London, 1813

About the Author

Stephen Mace was introduced to the study of sorcery in 1970, when a Tarot reading predicted an imminent disaster in his life. Three days later the State Police raided his apartment, confiscated his stock and trade, bound him with handcuffs, and locked him in their tomb/womb for six weeks. In the 35 years since he has dedicated himself to the discovery of the fundamental dynamics of the art, the better to empower individuals to defy the oppression of the State Apparatus. To this end he has written several books, those of greatest practical interest being *Stealing the Fire from Heaven, Shaping Formless Fire* and *Taking Power.*

MORE TITLES FROM STEPHEN MACE

SHAPING FORMLESS FIRE
Distilling the Quintessence of Magick

Magick is a psychic technology, a collection of observations about psychic energy and the techniques for manipulating it. *Shaping Formless Fire* presents these with a simple elegance that contradicts the notion that magick must remain a hidden art. There is psychic energy within us and all around us. We use its power to make our worlds, and to master it is to learn how to make the worlds we require. To see it as merely the way we perceive the world is to put ourselves at its mercy, and forfeit its power.

ISBN 1-56184-238-9

TAKING POWER
Claiming Our Divinity Through Magick

Taking Power offers a dynamic understanding of psychic power, and a vivid grasp of magick. From astral projection, the binding of spirits, power spots and the subtle body to the Holy Guardian Angel and magickal ethics, Mace presents it all in terms of the dynamics of psychic energy, without regard for any symbolic orientation. Thus the dynamics may be applied to any orientation, or to no orientation at all...

ISBN 1-56184-240-0

MORE BOOKS ON MAGIC

CONDENSED CHAOS
An Introduction to Chaos Magic
by Phil Hine
Foreword by Peter J. Carroll

"... the most concise statement ... of the logic of modern magic. Magic, in the light of modern physics, quantum theory and probability theory is now approaching science. We hope that a result of this will be a synthesis so that science will become more magical and magic more scientific."
— William S. Burroughs, author of *Naked Lunch*

"... a tour de force."— Ian Read, Editor, *Chaos International*

ISBN 1-56184-117-X

PRIME CHAOS
Adventures in Chaos Magic
by Phil Hine

An overview of the fastest-growing school of modern occultism: Chaos Magic. Simple, effective techniques for becoming proficient in practical magic, including ritual magic, sorcery, invocation, possession and evocation. *Prime Chaos* also explores some of the lighter—and darker—aspects of modern occultism, and presents new ideas for developing magical techniques.

"I wish I'd written this book!"
— Peter J. Carroll, author of *Liber Kaos* and *Psybermagick*

ISBN 1-56184-137-4

New Falcon Publications

Invites You to Visit Our Website:
http://www.newfalcon.com

At the Falcon website you can:

- Browse the online catalog of all of our great titles
- Find out what's available and what's out of stock
- Get special discounts
- Order our titles through our secure online server
- Find products not available anywhere else including:
    - One of a kind and limited availability products
    - Special packages
    - Special pricing
- Get free gifts
- Join our email list for advance notice of New Releases and Special Offers
- Find out about book signings and author events
- Send email to our authors (including the elusive Dr. Christopher Hyatt!)
- Read excerpts of many of our titles
- Find links to our author's websites
- Discover links to other weird and wonderful sites
- And much, much more

Get online today at http://www.newfalcon.com